THE
CLUB

A BROOKLYN LEGACY BY THE BAY

DANIELLE BERFOND

Copyright © 2025 Danielle Berfond
All rights reserved.
Published by Red Penguin Books
Bellerose Village, New York
Library of Congress Control Number: 2026905932
ISBN 978-1-63777-865-4 | 978-1-63777-866-1

No part of this book may be reproduced in any form or by any electronic or mechanical means, including information storage and retrieval systems, without written permission from the author, except for the use of brief quotations in a book review.

*For Grandma Gloria and Grandpa Bob, whose hard work and loyalty shaped our family - and so many others - and whose legacy lives on in ways they may never have imagined.
We miss you. Thank you.*

Table of Contents

FOREWORD VII
INTRODUCTION 01
THE BERFONDS & THEIR ACCIDENTAL 'PALMS SHORE CLUB' 06
    Bob the Builder 06
    Gloria the Matriarch 19

THE LAUNCH OF A BROOKLYN DESTINATION, 1960S AND
BEYOND 24
    The Summer Season 24
    The Cabana Boys: A Summer Dream Job 39
    The Pools: The Splashy Center of Action 46
    The Snack Bar: A Moving Heart 54
    Table Games: The Best Way to Spend A Summer Day 62
    Palms Shore Day Camp: Don't Forget the Kids 67
    The Switchboard: A Summer Soundtrack 72
    Wednesday Night Dinners: A Timeless Tradition with Offshoots . 76
    The 'Nightclub': From Day to Night 84
    A Place in the Action: Politics and the Palms 96
    A Teenage Home Base 104

THE 'HEY DAY' OF THE 1970S, EMBEDDING THE PALMS
IN BROOKLYN HISTORY 109
    A Tribute to the Community: Salute to Israel and Festa Italiana . 109
    The Unspoken: Mob Members at the Palms 114
    The Luau Room: From the World Fair to Disco Hideaway and
        Beyond 117
    The Berfonds Move In 121

A Rocky Relationship with the Neighborhood 123
A Spin-Off: The Palms Country Club 128

THE CHANGING TIMES OF THE 1980S AND 1990S 137
The Catering Era I: Every Affair is a Palms Affair 137
The Catering Era II: Allen & His Crew 144
A Berfond Wedding & Other Love Stories 151
Club PS: A Nightclub, 90s Style 157
A Supporting Cast of Characters. 161
A Slow Decline 168

EPILOGUE 173
ACKNOWLEDGEMENTS. 176

Foreword

It was early evening at City Bistro in Hoboken—the patio lights just coming on, the place buzzing softly—when a guy in a NYC JetSki jacket caught my eye. Something about him tugged at an old memory. I found myself asking, "Excuse me... do I know you?"

He turned and smiled. "I'm Brian. I run the JetSki tours from Hoboken Pier 13 to the Statue of Liberty."

We both did a double take.

"Brian??? Brian Orenstein!" I blurted. "From The Palms Shore Club! I haven't seen you in over 30 years!"

In an instant it all came rushing back—the two of us as twelve-year-olds at that little Sheepshead Bay summer oasis, pockets stuffed with quarters, waiting our turn to play Stargate in the arcade room. That chance meeting was five years ago now, and to this day we still laugh about those endless summer days. Our friends look at us like we're speaking another language, and maybe we are.

"They'll never know," we always say. No matter how much detail or context you give people who weren't lucky enough to experience the magical summers of The Palms Shore cabana club in Brooklyn, there's no way they'll understand the impact this mini Sheepshead Bay paradise had on our lives. So thank God for this book you're about to read!

The Palms was one of a kind—a true diamond in the rough. I can still see my grandma and Aunt Millie driving my sister and me there in their fabric-seat, light-blue '82 Oldsmobile, that giant red Playmate cooler wedged between us and packed with sandwiches, juices, and snacks for the day. A quick hop on and off the Belt Parkway and suddenly we were at the front door to another world. Beyond those gates was our escape from summer doldrums. Those long, hot July days were brutal, and relief was rare unless you ran through a lawn sprinkler or someone had that magical wrench to crack open the hydrant down the block. Nobody we knew had a pool. But the Palms did—two of them. One was Olympic-sized, the biggest pool I'd ever seen, and the other was fourteen feet deep with two diving boards that felt like cliffs to a kid.

For a child coming of age in the '80s, the Palms was freedom, a safe place to run wild from morning to dusk while the grown-ups relaxed, worry-free. For the adults, it was the ultimate daily social club, with a steady undercurrent of gossip and the occasional drama. Tea was spilled over low-stakes card games like Canasta, Mahjong and my Uncle Joe and Aunt Jennie's beloved Rummikub. Meanwhile, on the sun deck, tanned, shirtless, beer-bellied men smoking cigars played poker for higher stakes, just feet away from my mother, who was blissfully unaware, lost in her Sony Walkman as she baked in the sun overlooking the bay.

When I turned fourteen and was nudged toward earning my own money, the Palms was the obvious choice for my first summer job. Memorial Day weekend of 1988, I found myself behind the snack bar counter under Bob Berfond's watchful eye, serving coffee to friends, neighbors, and family. In the summers that followed, I took on more responsibility—first behind the snack bar, then in the catering hall, as the Palms quietly shaped the seasons of my adolescence.

Looking back now, I realize just how truly special they were. So, when I received a call from Allen Berfond—one of Bob and Gloria's three sons, the family that owned The Palms Shore Club—I felt a rush of excitement. He told me one of his daughters was writing a book about the club, and I could hardly believe it! A summer haven so near and dear to my heart was finally going to be documented, its memories preserved.

That mattered, because, at its core, The Palms was about families and friends. There was an undeniable sense of togetherness, a shared bond that connected everyone who passed through its gates. Parents, children, siblings, along with actual and honorary cousins, aunts and uncles gathered there summer after summer, under one roof. The cabanas weren't just shelters from the sun—they were where relationships deepened, friendships took root, and bonds were formed that lasted beyond the season. My parents made lifelong friends there. Some couples started businesses together. Others met their future spouses. And for me, it rekindled my childhood friendship with Brian.

So, I tip my cap to Danielle Berfond. In the pages ahead, she brings those memories to life—the faces, the names, the characters, the stories we all remember. For former cabana members, staff, and their families, long-forgotten tales will be confirmed and, through photographs, those magical moments will come rushing back. That summer feeling—the one we all remember—will roll in again, like it never left.

And for anyone who's only heard about The Palms Shore Club secondhand, get ready for a nostalgic dive into a time before social media and cell phone addiction—a time when every Memorial Day to Labor Day was reserved for fun, laughter, and sun at a Brooklyn slice of Americana. The Palms Shore Club.

– **Anthony Scire**, best known as **"Skeery Jones"**
Radio personality and executive producer
for Elvis Duran and the Morning Show on Z100 New York

INTRODUCTION

I can feel the sun on my back, the heat of the pavement beneath me, burning my legs just below my shorts. I lean over my lanyard, carefully threading the pink through the loop of blue in the box stitch, while subconsciously grabbing for a steak fry from the tray next to me. *Delicious*. I hear the *cawing* of the seagulls from the bay landing on the railing, a scream and then splash of a kid cannonballing off the diving board, the low hum of a cabana member's radio. The Palms Shore Club – my happy place.

I peer down from my concrete perch at the beautiful maze below: lounging, gossip-filled families who've made this Brooklyn pool club their summer home—swimming in the two vast pools, playing Mahjong or poker, dashing between the paddleball and tennis courts, or snacking while gazing out at the boats of Sheepshead Bay. Nearby, the distinctive rounded windows of the three-story event hall hint at another side of the Palms—where those same families trade their bikinis and swim shorts for dresses and suits to celebrate birthdays, weddings, and everything in between.

An aerial view of the Palms Shore Club in the 1990s (ignore the mark-up from some member of our family!)

The Palms Shore Club

View of the Palms Shore Club cabanas and patios from Sheepshead Bay in the 1970s

I love to be part of the crowd, but my introverted 10-year-old self also loves to escape to my secret hideaway, a slightly set-apart pavement terrace, one hand gripping a tray from the snack bar, another with my lanyard or book in hand, to spend some time alone. Perhaps, later, I will join Grandma Gloria back in her office to help with whatever tasks are at hand for the Palms Shore Club 1998 summer season. Or I may make my way into the adjoining catering hall and help my dad set the tables for this evening's wedding. I might even wander into the snack bar and ask if Grandpa Bob wants to play a round of rummy to see the smile on his typically gruff face that is reserved for his grandchildren.

Twenty-five years later, my memories are fading – blurring like the edges of a photograph, or like the view of Sheepshead Bay from my terrace perch in the summer haze. Still, spending my summer days at the Palms Shore Club was such an important part of my childhood. And, I know I am not the only one for whom this quirky but special place holds a deep significance.

INTRODUCTION

Over the years, I have been regaled with tales about the Palms from my parents, my aunts and uncles, my extended family, and even strangers I bump into in restaurants. I've seen the online posts from hundreds of people for whom the Palms was the backdrop for special occasions and favorite summer memories. At its core, the Palms was a cabana club—one of several that opened in the New York area during the mid-20th century, offering families a local escape for long summer days. Founded in 1962, it quickly became a beloved seasonal hub. But over time, I've come to understand that it was so much more than that.

I see the rich legacy of the Palms Shore Club, an evolving vision of my dad's father, my grandfather, Bob Berfond: a day-to-evening destination in the Brooklyn neighborhood of Sheepshead Bay, a sprawling complex of fun, food, and entertainment that could foster a true sense of community. It was the kingdom of my Grandpa Bob and Grandma Gloria, a place that grew into a vital gathering space at a time when community was everything.

The entrance to the Palms Shore Club in 1964 (courtesy of Barry Weinstein)

And I recognize now, how The Palms Shore Club is a piece of New York history, representing a vivid cross section of life in Brooklyn throughout those decades. It was a family cabana club by day, an elegant night club by evening and a rowdy dance club by night. Host to countless weddings and Sweet Sixteens, poker nights and ladies' lunches. At the center of it all was the Berfond family – my family.

It was my grandpa who built the Palms Shoes Club, so I feel a deep responsibility to preserve its story before it fades into memory. This is the time to do it: a few years ago, I sat listening and laughing with my dad and uncle as they reminisced of the Palms' early days, and it struck me how much history lived in their memories—and how few people remained to tell it. The Palms story had begun more than sixty years earlier, and time had blurred its edges for everyone who once called it their *summer home*.

So I began seeking out those who were there, while it was still possible. I listened to their stories, collected their photographs, tracked down old brochures and newspaper clippings, and tried to capture the essence and nostalgia of this unique place. What began as a personal project became something more—a record of a world that once existed along the Brooklyn coast. My hope is that this collection will keep that world alive, not only for future generations of my family, but for the broader Palms community and for anyone who longs to understand "the good old days" in Brooklyn.

At a time when our world has grown so vast and disconnected, I've come to appreciate how places like the Palms once offered something rare: a true sense of community and belonging, and the comforting feeling that you understood the world around you. So this book goes out to each of you—to everyone who lived in the neighborhood on Emmons Avenue, who worked as a cabana boy or waitress or lifeguard at the Palms Shore Club, who came to the evening shows or Salute to Israel festivals for a night out, who celebrated holidays or birthdays, who had your wedding and then your child's bat mitzvah there, who lazed by the pool or ate the free Wednesday night dinners.

And to any of you who had a similar experience at one of the other pool or beach clubs in the 60s, 70s, 80s, I hope this book helps you revive and relive some of those stories, as we take this walk down memory lane together.

Bob the Builder

THE BERFONDS & THEIR ACCIDENTAL 'PALMS SHORE CLUB'

My image of my Grandpa will always be of him sitting at one of the small square tables in the snack bar at the Palms: his light-blue short-sleeved striped shirt bulging at the pocket with a packet of cigarettes, as one dangled from his lips (lit or unlit); his very stiff white hat resting low on his forehead, tufts of white hair sticking out the side, matching his manicured white mustache; his piercing blue eyes, keenly observing his domain; and his ruddy face in a constant grimace – except when I bounded up to him. He would often be sitting with his friends, Palms fixtures Seymour or Larry G, silently overseeing the activities around him. I knew him to be a man of few words, though seeing me or my cousins would elicit a few more – and certainly more positive words – than he reserved for most others. Still, his form of affection was more often a rub of my ear, which I somehow both loved and hated. I was too young to see the visionary young contractor and entrepreneur, or the harsh but respected boss, that I have now learned him to be.

It was never part of Grandpa Bob's plan for him and his wife, my Grandma Gloria, to own and manage a cabana club, a nightclub, and an entertainment destination; to steer a business through four decades of change and to build a lasting Brooklyn legacy.

When he began the project that would become the Palms Shore Club in 1961, it was just another building job – though an important one. Through the 1950s, he had built a successful and prolific construction career with his brother Melvin, developing projects across

Brooklyn, particularly in the south and southeast neighborhoods of Canarsie, Mill Basin and Sheepshead Bay. Their uncle, Meyer Berfond, was an even more notable real estate mogul, and the two brothers were eager to make their own mark. Together, they built expansive shopping centers, scores of houses, and the towering apartment buildings many extended family and friends called home. They were building on the scale of New York real estate tycoons Fred Trump and Samuel J LeFrak. The Berfond brothers were an effective duo, Grandpa Bob the builder and Melvin 'the numbers guy', likely the brains of the outfit.

Along with their sister Sheila, they had grown up frugally – their parents Harry and Henrietta Berfond were from immigrant families. Harry had immigrated to the States as a child from Russia, and Henrietta's parents had come from Austria. Both came of age during the Depression, yet by the 1950s, their sons, Bob and Melvin, were on top of the world. When Grandpa Bob, just twenty-eight, married twenty-two-year-old Gloria Heiser in December 1956, he was able to throw a lavish wedding—complete with a video production that would rival any movie of the era.

But then, two years later tragedy struck. In 1958, Melvin died. And the empire they had been building was put on pause. Grandpa Bob was stuck with a lot of the financial obligations that Melvin had managed, and suddenly found himself under pressure from the banks and the mechanics. Eventually, he was forced to give up a lot of their properties, and while he soldiered on, his newer developments were on a smaller scale. Without his brother, and partner, business was never quite the same.

So when Grandpa got the call commissioning him to build this cabana club on Emmons Avenue, he welcomed the opportunity. He had a young family to take care of: a wife and two sons, my father, Allen, born in 1957 and Mel, my uncle, born in 1959 and named after Grandpa Bob's deceased brother. He developed the plans and led a construction team on this vast project, moving fast. He did have to work around some complications—one key hurdle being a building that stood in the way of his vision: the Miramar Yacht Club. Grandpa Bob made them a deal. We may never know the specifics of the back and forth, but in essence, he would build them a new Yacht Club on a different piece of property down the block (which still stands today).

He wanted to make sure this new project would become something special – and it certainly was. With its unique, Art-Deco-adjacent architecture,

Grandma Gloria and Grandpa Bob at their wedding in 1956

tall oblong windows, arched roof, and tan stucco finish, it stood out from everything else on Emmons Avenue. The impressive project was completed in June 1962. And that should have been it.

But things change. The group that had commissioned the club pulled out, leaving Grandpa Bob holding the bag. All of a sudden, with two young sons and Grandma Gloria pregnant with their third child, he found himself with a sprawling complex on his hands. They were living in a modest two-bedroom apartment on Nostrand Avenue, just a short drive from the property, and though it should have felt overwhelming, they saw an opportunity instead.

In true Berfond entrepreneurial fashion—armed with little more than grit and blind faith—they decided to take the leap. Grandpa Bob lived by the maxim, "why not?"

He pushed forward, catapulting the entire family into a business he knew nothing about. With Grandma Gloria by his side—and an extended family of siblings, cousins, and friends ready to play their

Selection of photos from the well-documented construction of the Palms Shore Club in May and June 1962 (continued on following pages)

parts—he stepped into the unknown. He didn't have experience, but he had confidence. And that was enough to begin. In 1962, a year after their third son, Larry, was born, their other "baby," the Palms Shore Club, opened its doors.

It would turn out that the risk was worth the reward. Grandpa Bob's vision filled a need for community space in Sheepshead Bay, a neighborhood in southern Brooklyn named after the small body of water that separates it from its more famous neighbor, Coney Island, and from the Atlantic Ocean. Sheepshead Bay was changing in the early 1960s. The neighborhood had seen ups and downs over the years, but by the 1960s, the previously quiet area was quickly developing – with a boom in residential buildings and a growing middle-class community of Jewish and Italian families eager to take advantage of the waterfront.

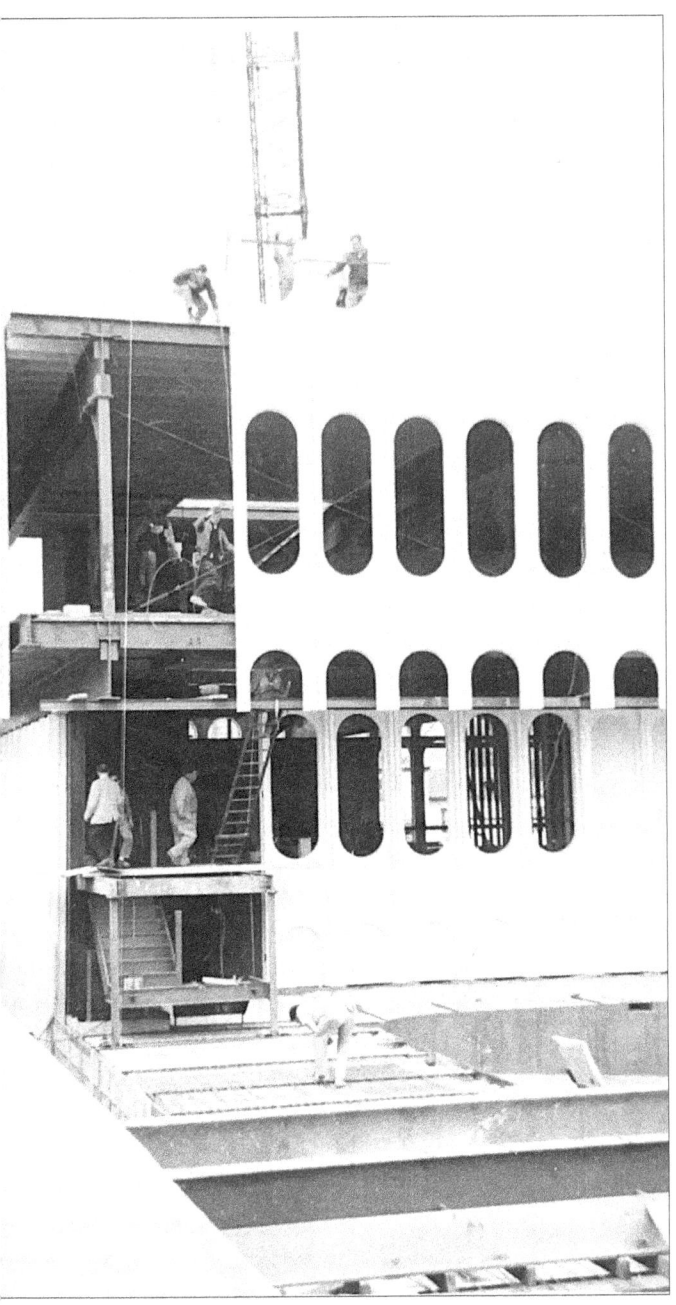

Here the Palms Shore Club found its place. It stood on Emmons Avenue, the main thoroughfare, running along the bay with piers for private boats and restaurants like the famous Lundy's, known for its seafood, and later my favorite, Roll-n-Roaster, the retro fast-food spot loved for its roast beef sandwiches.

The Palms Shore Club

Cabana clubs were becoming a popular place to gather and graze in the hot summer months across the New York region, particularly for families that couldn't or didn't want to make the trek Upstate to the Catskills (historically a haven for city dwellers). Yet, there were only a handful of cabana clubs in Brooklyn for local families to take advantage of. In Sheepshead Bay, it was really just the Deauville Beach club on Knapp Street; and in neighborhoods beyond, the El Caribe, the Silver Gull and the Brighton Beach Baths.

New York Times article in June 1962 on building surge in Sheepshead Bay, referencing the near-completion of the Palms Shore Club

At Sheepshead Bay: Prosperity Increases and Population Rises in a Nautical Corner of Brooklyn

Emmons Avenue runs along the shore of Sheepshead Bay in southern part of Brooklyn · Fishing vessels, many for hire for deep-sea or bottom fishing, tied at piers on the avenue

Boom in Brooklyn

In Quiet Sheepshead Bay the Tide Has Turned Again, With Mixed Results

By BERNARD WEINRAUB

The Palms Shore Club reflects the prosperity of the area · Apartment buildings are replacing shacks on Bragg Street

New York Times article in February 1966 on Sheepshead Bay neighborhood evolution, highlighting the Palms Shore Club

Grandpa Bob's Palms Shore Club quickly met the growing demand. At the heart of its 60,000-square-foot, multi-level waterfront campus were two crystal-clear, blue swimming pools: an Olympic-sized main pool on the lower deck, and nearby on the upper deck, a fourteen-foot–deep diving tank. Between the pools and Emmons Avenue stood a three-story hall with grand entry stairs and large

THE KINGDOM OF BERFOND **THE PALMS SHORE CLUB**

In a world influenced by ideologies and governments, there stands one entity with no other parralell -- THE PALMS SHORE CLUB. Most people are familiar with Marxism, Leninism, socialism and capitalism, but only a few selected citizens recognize BERFONDISM. The theory of Berfondism is not you run of the mill philosopyn. It is the written and unwritten laws of Bob Berfond that keeps the delicate harmony, between members, owners and employees in balance.

In the constitution of the Palms, written on July 1, 1962 there were 2 basic articles that has guided this entity to its dominant position in world Cabana Clubs. ARTICLE I-Sec. 1 Every customer shall be honored, respected and allowed to persue his own happiness.

Sec. 2 Service by all employees shall be quick, clean and trustworthy -- with no exceptions.

Sec. 3 It would be with the appreciation of the management if all violations of the above sections were reported to any Berfond.

ARTICLE II Sec. 1 In order to form the perfect government in our society, the Palms has chosen the very organized and efficient system of hegemonic rule.

Sec. 2 Our world at the Palms shall be divided into 3 separate city-states. The front gate, swithboard and rentals; the snack bar; and the cabanas, lockers and pool.

Sec. 3 Each of these city-states shall be under the jurisdictions of one governor.

Sec. 4. These three governors will have the complete control over their soveriegn territory until a problem arises or a correction must be made. When these situations become apparent, the governors will have to answer and obey the supreme decisions of the KING. THIS man will have final say in all matters concerning the very complex world of the PALMS SHORE CLUB.

First page of a 'manifesto' to the Berfond kingdom, which our family uncovered in a box of Palms Shore Club mementos (date and author unknown) windows overlooking the club. Surrounding the pools on the other three sides were long rows of side-by-side cabanas with chairs and terraces that looked out over either the pools or the boats in the bay. From cabanas on the east, guests could watch the action on the paddleball, handball, and basketball courts.

Over the years, there would be expansions and renovations, but this remained the core layout for the four decades the Palms Shore Club was in operation: the pools and patios alive with energy during the summer days, and the elegant hall hosting celebrations and nightlife year-round.

My grandparents had been married only a few years when the Palms Shore Club was born, so they started this journey together. From literally nothing, they built not only the infrastructure, but the community, the story, the legacy of the Palms. They were characters who didn't always do things "by the book," but they invested themselves completely in the business, constantly innovating and evolving. They did it with gusto, and—at least for Grandma Gloria— often with a smile. Grandpa Bob was the visionary, especially in the beginning, the public face and voice of the Palms; Gloria was the rock, balancing Bob's fiery temperament and ensuring all ran smoothly.

Grandpa Bob wasn't a conventional businessman, or a conventional boss. He could be charming when he wanted to be, particularly when promoting the Palms in its early days. But those who really knew him often referred to him – relatively affectionately – as "Tyrone Wildcat," a nickname coined by cabana boy Steven M to capture the tyrant within him. He wasn't chatty, usually sporting a silent and unapproachable grimace, but when he did engage, he had a wry sense of humor and wasn't what you'd call politically correct. There wasn't a phony bone in his body. His sharp blue eyes were often shaded by a hat or peeking from beneath his infamous toupee, missing nothing. He had a quick temper, and everyone, from the oldest members to the youngest cabana boys, knew you couldn't pull one over on him.

Grandpa Bob was dedicated to his creation, and he demanded the same from those who worked for him. He could be tough—it was

his way or the highway. He was quick to yell (loudly), accuse someone of stealing or slacking, or fire an employee on the spot, though he might later forget or be persuaded to hire them back. (Some, like Steve Finkelstein or Ronald Kestenbaum, were fired and rehired multiple times). If he was angry, he never hesitated to dress someone down in front of others. These behaviors, likely learned from his own father, trickled through to his sons, though have softened with time. Despite this gruffness, there was deep respect and even affection for "Tyrone." Not only from his few favorites who escaped his ire, but from those who endured it. They understood that this "tough love" was part of his nature—a kind of education, a way of building resilience. Even his own brand of motivation. And it worked. Many of the young men in particular who worked their way through the Palms

A caricature of Grandpa Bob drawn by longtime Palms member Cary Mitnick

credit Grandpa Bob with teaching them valuable life skills— even if some lessons were about what *not* to do.

Grandpa Bob's affection came slowly, and wasn't always obvious, but that only made it more meaningful when it came. People sensed the soft heart beneath the hard shell and cared deeply what he thought of them. When he believed in someone—when he promoted a cabana boy, delegated a responsibility, or stepped in when someone was upset—it meant everything.

Perhaps, his greatest expression of affection was teaching someone how to gamble. His younger cousins, his sons and their friends, his nephew, and eventually his grandchildren – all were imparted with Grandpa Bob's gambling skills, usually through gin-rummy or horse betting. He seemed happiest in the quiet concentration of a card game among his closest family and friends.

Yet this downtime was rare, especially in the early years. Everyone saw how hard he worked and how much of himself he invested. While

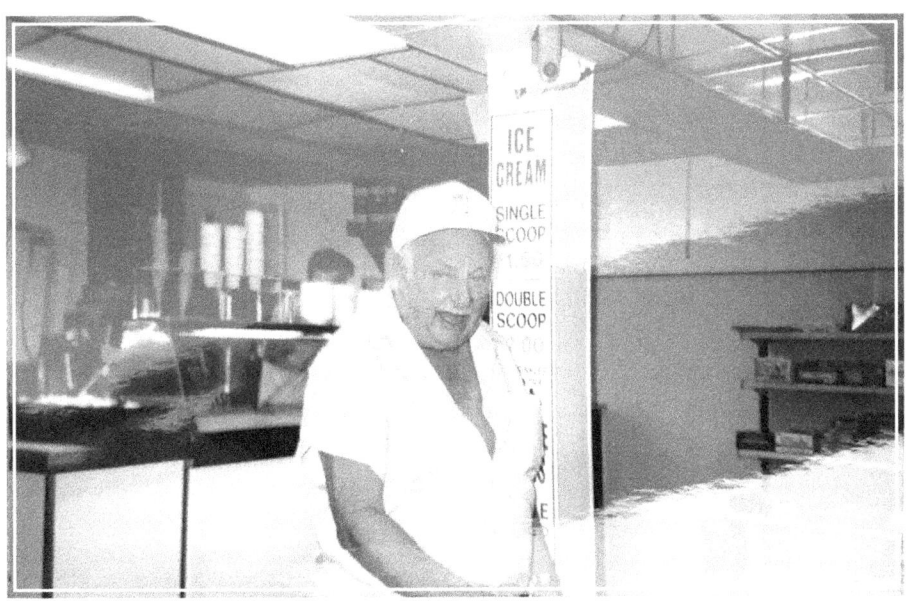

Grandpa Bob in the snack bar in the early 1990s
(see the resemblance to the caricature above!)

there were many wonderful, trusted staff at the Palms, Grandpa Bob stayed actively involved until his sons were old enough to take over different parts of the business. On weekends, he'd stay late to oversee the nightclub upstairs and show up bleary-eyed the next morning to supervise the snack bar, cigarette dangling, demanding a coffee. He put in the work, and expected others to do the same. A work ethic that defined the Palms, and ensured a quality experience that kept staff and guests coming year after year, generation after generation.

Gloria the Matriarch

I can still picture her, Grandma Gloria. Beautiful, strong, stately, always impeccably put together, her hair cleanly yet softly pulled back in a way that somehow embodied her gentle but unmistakable authority. At times charming, at times stern, I knew from a young age that Gloria Berfond was a force to be reckoned with—the matriarch not only for our Berfond clan but of the entire Palms community. She always had a proud smile for me, which I sought to earn. I loved being her right-hand helper: laminating the membership cards, filing papers at the imposing desk in her original wood-paneled office, doing whatever was needed as she bragged about me and my cousins to the members.

I could see how they respected her, how they sought to be her friend. She was warm yet professional, and at times slightly distant, the queen of this kingdom that she and my grandfather created.

Grandma Gloria in the final incarnation of the snack bar in the 1990s

From the beginning, Grandma Gloria was a true partner to Grandpa Bob. She and her older brother, Arnold, and younger sister, Lois, were all incredibly bright, raised by intellectual parents, Hyman Heiser, an engineer turned real estate salesman, and Sadie, probably one of the most well-read housewives of her time. Grandma Gloria was valedictorian of her high school class in Elmont, New York, and while still uncommon in the 1950s for women to attend college, she took accounting courses and later landed a job with an architecture firm. That job turned out to be a twist of fate: it was her boss who set her up on a blind date with Bob Berfond.

By many accounts, Grandma Gloria was out of his league and she impressed him further with her beauty, brains, and sophisticated audacity. She was not your average Jewish girl, ordering a beer on their first date (in a glass, of course, because she always kept it classy). Bob's ambition and achievements at such a young age ultimately drew her in. After a brief courtship, they were married in 1956, in an extravagant wedding that allowed him to show off both his professional and personal success. At just twenty-two-years old – six years younger than her new husband – Grandma Gloria immediately put her intellect to work, helping with the books for Grandpa Bob's construction business (and later for the Palms itself) while also starting to grow their family.

After the Palms Shore Club opened, her role expanded. She became the matron of the cabana-club community. A few years in, she took charge of managing the members—signing up new families and, over the years, handling both their accounts and their personalities. She'd sit in her office or at the entrance, sometimes with one of her young sons (most often shy Mel) quietly at her side, greeting members as they arrived while mentally calculating their balances

Grandma Gloria welcoming members in 1992

or tracking their guest passes. She was smart and direct, yet pleasant and fair, the person members could come to with their complaints, requests and stories, the ones they wouldn't dare bring to Grandpa Bob. Grandma Gloria knew how to get things done, and she always knew what was going on. Like the time young Alan Horowitz, in his pre-cabana boy days, accidentally locked a few members in a cabana then feigned innocence to all around, except Grandma Gloria, who saw right through him, eliciting a confession.

Her role went beyond just managing the people. Grandma Gloria was the one who cultivated the sense of community—the magic that made the Palms a special place to be.

She planned activities, games and contests that kept members engaged; she oversaw the Day Camp that entertained the kids so the adults could relax; and she developed newsletters that both informed and - fueled the chatter every thriving community needs. The gossip and goings-on were captured in the elaborately printed *Tattler* newspaper in the 1960s and the more informal *Down By The Palms* compilations in the 1970s and 80s. And Grandma Gloria kept the engine of this wonderful chaos humming. With her steady hand, the Palms Shore Club became a true destination, with a warmth and family feel that clubs like the Deauville, the Silver Gull, or the El Caribe couldn't match. It wasn't just a business or a place to go; it was a summer home. The Palms was big enough to offer variety for adults and adventure for children, but small enough for everyone to know one another—to see familiar faces day after day and build real community. One year, the children even performed a jingle set to a calypso tune:

The El Caribe may be very big with cabanas extra plush,
But where else but the Palms Shore Club could you find people just like us?
'The Palms is, Ooh, Better'.

It was this vibe that not only drew so many members in, but kept them coming back, decade after decade.

Grandma Gloria was an effective partner and the perfect counterbalance to Grandpa Bob's fiery nature. That's not to say it was always smooth sailing. Their lives centered around the Palms Shore Club, with little separation between personal and professional, save for their Monday evening family outings to the racetrack or dinner. The intensity could take a toll. Add to that two strong-willed, stubborn personalities, and sparks were inevitable. They wouldn't raise their voices, but arguments could lead to prolonged silent treatment – days or even weeks of not speaking, using their sons as go-betweens. The tension could permeate the whole club. Yet, like everything else about them, this fighting too became part of the Palms' character, a familiar quirk of any extended family.

Running a thriving business while raising three sons, Grandma Gloria quickly earned the respect and admiration of members – and perhaps even more so, of the women who worked at the Palms. At the cabana club, the lines were clear – Grandma Gloria managed

Grandma Gloria and Grandpa Bob passing out bagel breakfasts in the 1960s

the women, and Grandpa Bob managed the men. She oversaw the women who ran the camp or manned the switchboard; those who helped with bookkeeping, like Myra and Rose; and those who assisted in her office with paperwork and member tours, like Cindy Solomon, Hilarie, and Stephanie Berk Wilner. When there was a single cabana 'girl' (Liz Streeter) or the first female lifeguards, they were inevitably placed under her supervision. Even those who didn't report to Grandma Gloria directly, like the waitresses and snack bar staff, felt her presence. She was a mentor, a role model, an example of intelligence and composure.

In the 1960s and '70s, when few women held leadership roles, Grandma Gloria stood out as a capable, confident and respected figure others could look up to. As kind as she was, she could be firm when needed and never tolerated disrespect. But, if you worked hard, she treated you fairly, more than fairly. Beyond the staff, even performers and longtime members valued her steady support.

She was beloved by many at the Palms, who often thought of her and Grandpa Bob as close friends. Yet she kept those relationships professional, maintaining a healthy distance even with those staff and members who adored her. Her closest friend was Grandpa Bob's sister, my great-aunt Sheila Weinberg, who filled many roles at the Palms, pitching in wherever needed. Aunt Sheila was her right-hand, spending hours in the office with Grandma Gloria, helping with paperwork, managing members and brainstorming how to negotiate with the men. Those skills were quietly absorbed by her youngest daughter, Melissa, who spent her days observing the two women at work. The baby of that generation, Melissa was eager to help her strong female role models however she could, running to the snack bar to fetch them coffee or lunch, and carrying messages to various family members working in different locations around the club. She was a devoted little deputy.

Grandma Gloria and Aunt Sheila were inseparable, practically sisters themselves, and Sheila became an important confidante to Grandma Gloria as she navigated the triumphs and trials of building this Brooklyn landmark.

The Summer Season

THE LAUNCH OF A BROOKLYN DESTINATION, 1960s AND BEYOND

We all remember our first job. Mine? Laminating membership cards for the Palms summer season. And at seven-years-old, I took this job very seriously. I remember sitting in my Grandma Gloria's cozy wood-paneled office, my small legs swinging under the bulky desk, as I slid the printed cards into the clear plastic pouches and slowly guided them through the humming laminating machine. I'd then carefully use a paper cutter to trim the still-warm pouches down to size, enjoying the satisfying 'whoosh' as the blade sliced the plastic. Later I'd take the pile to my grandma, and stand proudly by her side as she handed these brand-new membership cards over to long-time patrons, who were eager for the new summer season to begin.

The physical membership cards changed over the decades, but from the day the doors opened in the summer of 1962, they acted as the keys that unlocked a summer of fun. From Memorial Day to Labor Day each year, the Palms Shore Club was a place where

Palms Shore Club membership card from 1969, with hole punches for days spent at the Club (courtesy of Carol Notias Lambos)

the increasing number of middle-class families in south Brooklyn passed their summer days. It was a place where women could soak up the sun and relax with friends; where children could be happily occupied with the day camp or swimming; where teenagers could show off and flirt, perhaps get their first job; where men could come join their families after work or on weekends, and play sports or cards with their buddies.

As its name implies, central to the Palms cabana club were the rows of connected cabanas that members rented for the season. These small rooms were essentially home base—a place to store your belongings, towels, and kids' toys so you didn't have to schlep them back and forth from home every day; a private spot to shower, cool off from the blazing sun, or wait out the rain; and a designated meeting point where friends and family knew where to find you for a game or gossip. Each cabana came with lounge chairs and mats for sunbathing. Members could choose a full or half cabana and whether to share across families. The rates, starting at around $500 in the early 1960s, were reasonable for a daily destination, but still a commitment. Prices also varied by location: the most expensive cabanas were on the upper decks overlooking the pool or the bay. Those coveted spots often required years on a waitlist, with members "graduating" up the tiers over time.

There was also a less expensive option: individuals or couples could rent lockers for the summer to store their belongings and reserve lounge chairs (and umbrellas, if desired) on the decks. These "deck dwellers" or "sun worshippers" had a culture of their own. They would stake out spots among the neatly aligned rows of lounge chairs, often returning to the same area day after day, plopping themselves down for hours – aided by baby oil, or tanning lotion, and the occasional foil reflector.

Beyond the cabanas and lockers, membership cards granted access to a range of amenities: the pools, of course, and the sports courts for tennis, volleyball, shuffleboard, handball, and a fan favorite, paddleball. The paddleball courts were where kids learned to play and adults, young and old, competed in tournaments against

The Palms Shore Club

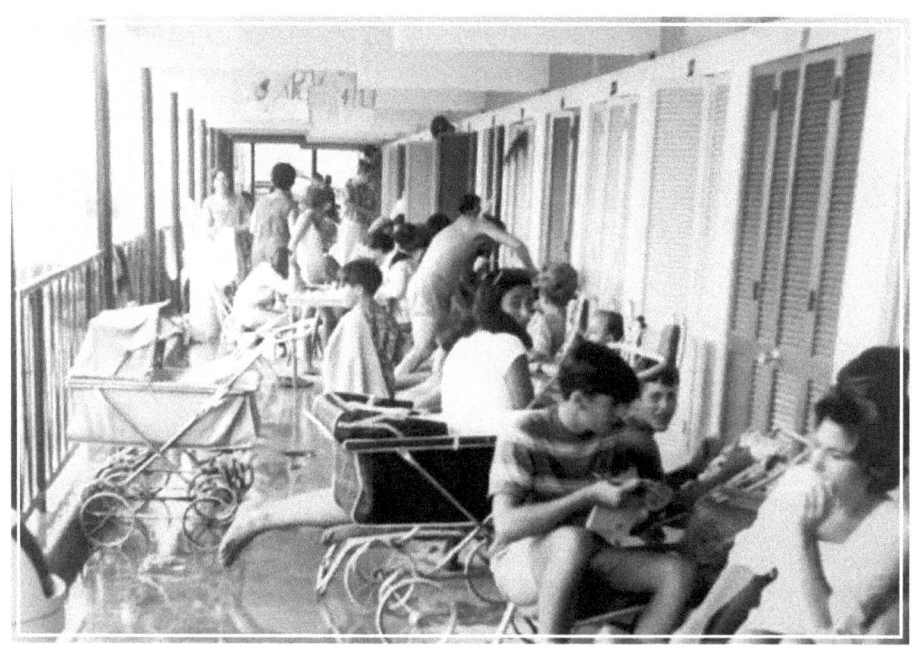

Busy cabanas on the jokingly-termed "diaper row" in the 1960s (photo by Morris Shrem)

A peek inside the cabanas behind my cousins, after a day in the pool! Left to right, and back to front: Nicole, Jenine holding Lindsey, Jackie, Danielle (me!), and Jake

one another and other beach clubs, mostly good-naturedly. Some men spent entire weekend days (between naps) bouncing balls off of those concrete walls. For less competitive members, there was access to the dance studio, gym, sauna, and salon – all added over time. In the 1960s, dedicated activities directors organized slates of fun for all age groups.

```
PALMS SHORE CLUB              1128 Emmons Avenue                    SH 3-4444

        SCHEDULE OF RATES                           SUMMER 1967

   EAST CABANA -----------  TERRACE WEST -----------  POOL WEST 1-6      $900.00
                            6 People . . . . . . . $150.00 each
                            7 People . . . . . . .  140.00 each
                            8 People . . . . . . .  130.00 each

   TERRACE EAST ---------  TERRACE POOL EAST 1-6  --------  TERRACE POOL WEST 1-6   $930.00
                            6 People . . . . . . . $155.00 each
                            7 People . . . . . . .  145.00 each
                            8 People . . . . . . .  135.00 each

   WEST CABANA ----------  POOL WEST 9-14  ----------  POOL EAST 1-8     $990.00
                            6 People . . . . . . . $165.00 each
                            7 People . . . . . . .  155.00 each
                            8 People . . . . . . .  145.00 each

   POOL WEST 15-22 ------  POOL EAST 9-28 ---------  TERRACE POOL EAST 7-34  $1110.00
                            6 People . . . . . . . $185.00
                            7 People . . . . . . .  175.00
                            8 People . . . . . . .  165.00

        RATES PER CABANA MEMBER FOR MORE THAN 6 ADULTS WILL ONLY BE EFFECTIVE IF THE
   CABANA IS RENTED IN FULL. Each Child will be charged 1/2 price membership regardless
   of age of child. Children enrolled in day camp will not be counted in cabana count.

            LOCKER RENTAL . . . . . . . . . . . . $135.00 one person
                                                  $240.00 two people

            WEEK-END LOCKER (FOR HUSBANDS OF MEMBERS ONLY) ............ $85.00

            CHAISE LOUNGE RENTAL . . . . . . . . . . . . . $25.00

            UMBRELLA RENTAL . . . . . . . . . . . . . . .  20.00

        ALL RATES SUBJECT TO NEW YORK STATE 5% TAX.

              * * * * * * * * * * * * * * * * * * * * * * * *

            DAY CAMP (Children 3-8) Six days (Mondays Off) .......... $150.00
                    Included transportation to Club
```

Summer membership rates for the Palms Shore Club in 1967

The Palms Shore Club

Our plans for 1968 include expanding the Sundecks. This will mean far more reserved lounges will be available for your comfort. To insure everyone of having a chair, we have therefore reduced the price of the Lounges to $20.00 per lounge.

There was also regularly scheduled entertainment – most often musical acts but also local events Grandpa Bob offered to host. In its second year, the Palms hosted the finals of the *Miss Brooklyn* contest, a beauty pageant sponsored by *The Brooklyn Eagle* newspaper. At a time when such contests were quite a local sensation, *Miss Brooklyn* brought both people and attention to the new Palms venue.

While these newsworthy moments stood out, daily life at the Palms was a steady stream of amusing activities for all ages. Mother-daughter look-a-like competitions, watermelon-eating contests, dance lessons to master disco-era Hustle moves; voting for Miss and Mrs. and Mr. Palms Shore Club (like long-time member Al Pantoch) and other silly superlatives; talent shows and demonstrations, such as father-and-son duo Jack and Lee Stern showing off karate skills — using swords to slice cucumbers in half on each other's neck and stomachs, to the crowd's delight. There was always something going on.

Members hanging on the packed patios in the 1960s, sunning themselves, playing cards and overlooking Sheepshead Bay

The Palms Shore Club

Members playing on the popular paddleball courts on Labor Day 1987, as captured in video footage of the Palms for the holiday

Perhaps most importantly, those membership cards granted access to a *community*. A community of fellow Brooklynites – up to 1,500 members at the Palms' peak – with whom you could forge friendships or deepen existing ones as you spent long days together, swimming, gossiping, laughing, and lounging. Bonds were formed during games and pranks, in lines for the free Wednesday night dinners, and over paddleball rivalries. Many members came with family and friends, but countless others left with new lifelong friendships, or even met their future partners, thanks to the Palms.

Of course, there would still be spats. Gather that many people under the hot summer sun, and tempers could flare—over deck chairs, paddleball games, or nothing at all. But those fights usually blew over as quickly as they began, family-style disagreements forgotten the next day.

The Brooklyn Eagle article from June 1963, describing the new Palms Shore Club, the venue of the Miss Brooklyn contest finals

The Palms Shore Club

HAVING A WONDE[RFUL TIME]

Congenial company makes the Wednesday Line more pleasant.

An extra treat for Wednesday Night was a glass of Carousel Wine

We welcome you to our home away from home

The name of the game is Canasta

A happy family circle at the Palms

The Summer Season

A spread in the Palms Shore Tattler in 1968 capturing the spirit of the cabana club community

The Palms Shore Club

One of the many advertisements for the Palms Shore Club

Even if you didn't know *everyone*, the Palms Shore Club felt safe and familiar. Within its gates, parents trusted that others would look after their children – other mothers shared snacks or lent lunch money, lifeguards and cabana boys jumped in to help if needed. It was a home-away-from-home, free from the worries and anxieties of the outside world.

The deep sense of community and constant fun created a little envy among those in the neighborhood who weren't members, and guest passes were in high demand. Members sometimes "miscounted" their guests or tried to sneak in a friend using someone else's card. So membership cards and guest passes had to be checked diligently at the front gate by a designated guard or two stationed behind the infamous industrial metal desk—the same one used for decades, squeakily rolled out each morning and back inside each evening, repainted so many times the drawers barely opened and the wheels barely turned.

In the early years, when membership cards listed only names and no photos, it was quite the task to manage the gate—you had

The Summer Season

Poem about the start of summer at the Palms, by longtime member Alice Yallowitz, which our family uncovered in a box of Palms Shore Club mementos

to know everyone by sight. Lou P was the best at the job, with a photographic memory that allowed him to recall every member's name, face, family, and even their car as they pulled up. His front-gate partner, Grandpa's cousin "Big Larry" Berfond, could skate by.

After Lou and Larry, Grandma Gloria often took on the front gate role, rotating with others, including her sons. Adding photos to the cards made the job easier, but didn't prevent the inevitable: lost cards, forgotten cards, or ones ruined in the washing machines (in the pre-lamination days). Grandma knew every member by name and face, but anyone who showed up without a card could still expect a grilling. A true member was rarely turned away, but if an unsanctioned guest snuck in, Grandma was furious (even if Grandpa Bob was likely to spot them and chase them out). It was all a testament to the Palms' becoming the summer place to be.

Part of that draw was the beautiful, well-kept premises, for which Grandpa Bob took full responsibility. In the lead-up to and during each season, he ensured the entire campus met his exacting standards. Grandpa Bob had a few particular obsessions, starting with the pools. He insisted that they remain pristine, the centerpiece of his vision, though he rarely, if ever, went in. Every year, before the Memorial Day opening, he would have handymen spend hours in the drained basins, first using grinders to slowly scrape and smooth the sides, then repainting them a brilliant blue with special paint imported from New Jersey.

The pool borders were almost as important to Grandpa Bob, leading to his second obsession: concrete! Even a hairline crack on the decks was unacceptable; he would direct his men to break up and repour the entire areas. One of his happiest days – perhaps rivalling his wedding or the births of his three sons – was when he purchased his own concrete mixer. He used it within an inch of its life.

Less thrilling to Grandpa Bob, but just as vital, was the annual spring repainting of every single surface. Tweens were often recruited as unpaid helpers for the tedious prep – delicately taping newspapers over 200 cabana mirrors to protect them when the painters came through. Altogether, it was quite the annual undertaking. Yet the meticulous repairs and refreshes, along with constant maintenance throughout the season, kept the Palms pristine and comfortable for everyone.

The end of each summer season, Labor Day, was always bittersweet. It was, for many, one of the best days of the year: a chaotic celebration of water balloons, shaving cream fights, pranks, and people tossed into the pool. Cabana boys and snack-bar workers eagerly awaited the "end of season" tips from members. But it was also a sad day, for members and staff alike. Their summer family would disperse across Brooklyn and beyond, not to reunite for another nine months.

This family evolved over time, but many considered the Palms their summer home for decades – staying through the multiple eras of music and fashions and sports. Generations of families like the Pantochs, the Urbans and the Tischlers.

No matter how much changed within and beyond the Palms Shore Club from 1962 to 1999, what remained consistent was that the cabana club was a summer home to its members and staff.

Bay News article from August 1981, capturing the extensive goings-on at the Palms Shore Club

The Cabana Boys: A Summer Dream Job

I just remember how cool they looked to my nine-year-old eyes. The teenage boys confidently striding around the Palms, saying hello to the members, joking around with each other, flirting with all of the girls, all while skillfully balancing trays of food or easily rearranging the heavy chairs. The cabana boys were the subject of many conversations with my older cousins, who would debate who was the cutest and vie for their attention – though we all knew that Grandpa Bob would never allow them to get near his granddaughters. Still, it didn't hurt to look.

Cabana boys were the engine of the Palms Shore Club from its opening. Members came during the summer to relax and have fun; the cabana boys were there to make sure they didn't have to lift a finger. These were mostly high-school and college-aged boys

A cabana boy hard at work, ringing up a tray of lunches for the members in his row, in 1987

from the neighborhood, and the occasional girl in later years, looking for a gig for a few summers. This was a pretty coveted job, most often reserved for those with an "in" – friends of the Berfond boys or extended family or children of long-time Palms members. Once hired by Grandpa Bob, cabana boys were paired up and designated one or two of the twelve or so rows of small cabanas, coined by their location in the club (say, Pool East or Terrace West). They would *schlep* out all of the wooden lounge chairs and mats and folding tables and chairs each morning, and in the evening, they'd pack them away and tidy up the cabana and surrounding area. Most importantly, cabana boys fetched a never-ending cycle of food for members throughout the day, so they didn't need to leave their Mahjong game or tanning position.

Lowest on the cabana boy totem pole were the "deck boys". There were many people who would lounge and play cards beyond the cabanas, out on the sundecks and pool patios – in particular the locker-only members but also day guests or cabana-holders who liked to switch up their environments. So the "deck boys" were responsible for dragging around mats for the loungers and running for their lunches and drinks. Without a dedicated row of cabanas and therefore cabana members, their experiences and tip-base were much less consistent – but it was a starting point. One quarter per mat, for example, could quickly add up. Part of Palms lore is that Harvey Keitel – the Brighton Beach native who became an award-nominated actor and Martin Scorsese favorite – was a deck boy those first summers in the 1960s. While Harvey did not stay on – he had movies to make! – many others who started in this position worked their way up to becoming cabana boys, and to the better cabana rows, over time.

Though perhaps there was one lower-rung role: water boy. This was the first job for Grandpa Bob's eleven-year-old nephew, Philip Weinberg. A pitcher filled with ice water in one small hand, a stack of small paper cups in the other, he would weave his skinny body in between lounge chairs all around the crowded club, offering the cool refreshment to members. It was a welcome reprieve during the hot summer day, and the dime or quarter tips would accumulate quickly in Philip's pockets. A preview for his later years as a full-fledged cabana boy.

The cabana boys worked hard, but it was also a dream job for the young men, who eagerly came back year after year – often until they went away to college or a full-time job. They didn't make regular wages, so the cabana boys relied on tips from members in their rows; but they were still handsomely rewarded. It was an unspoken norm that members should tip on a weekly basis – most often on Sundays – as well as for food brought during the week. The cabana boys would make sure they were at their posts on Sunday evenings to gather their tips, like Ronald Kestenbaum sitting on the railing to ensure no one in his row left without ponying up. The teenagers would then walk home, perhaps over-confidently, pockets stuffed with one-dollar bills. But there was a wide spectrum of generosity. Some individual members were known for being the best tippers, from a few successful businessmen like Duke to some of the sweet older ladies. There were even 'better' cabana rows, with the more expensive cabanas, where members were looser with their wallets and generally more easy-going. At the beginning of the summer, the cabana boys vied heavily for these assignments – while generally based on tenure, there were some exceptions, leading to a decent amount of envy among the group.

The 'cheaper' members would get their own food from the snack bar or just not tip at all, and then hand a few measly dollars on Sunday. Some cabana boys were not shy about their frustration with these members, essentially holding them hostage at the cabanas to demand tips, or going as far as to mess with the cabanas in retribution. Paul Rosenblit once tossed a check back at a large-group table after a non-existent tip, and received a light smack on the back of the head and requisite tongue-lashing from Grandpa Bob in return (Grandpa was equally intolerant of stingy cabana members and misbehaving cabana boys). And the cabana boys wouldn't want to leave their posts before members left on Sunday, in fear of missing their tips – even if it meant risking Grandpa Bob's wrath if they didn't shift to other responsibilities. Fortunately, most members were both timely and generous, and the teenagers could earn quite a tidy sum over the summer.

Especially on Labor Day weekend, when – weather permitting – the cabana boys could make a killing on end-of-season tips (at least from those members who didn't sneak out the last day). They would also flag down any final payment from Grandpa Bob, including the promised amount for each Wednesday night dinner worked. He would infamously procrastinate paying his staff, doing so begrudgingly and inconveniently (cabana boy Barry Weinstein remembers once getting over $100 in pennies in a bank bag). In total, Labor Day weekend could be one of the most lucrative weekends of the season, sometimes enough by itself to cover a semester of college tuition.

But it was still tip-dependent. In the '80s, Grandpa Bob did relent a bit, and decided to give the cabana boys $100 for the summer so they had some certainty – but only if they wore Palms t-shirts and hats every day, a definite change from the previously quite loose dress code. It wouldn't have been a big deal, but the cheap foam hats were far from comfortable, sweaty and itchy during the long, hot and sunny days. One day, Eddie Reavan led his fellow cabana boys in a hat rebellion: call it courageous or stupid, but he stood up to Bob, asserting that the hats were not a good idea. Yet even before Eddie finished, seeing Grandpa Bob's face turn red, the other teenagers had started slinking back. Eddie was on his own – bearing the brunt of Grandpa screaming and threatening his job. For several more years, the hats as well as the t-shirts were an established and uncontested uniform.

The cabana boys took away a lot more than money from these summers. For most of the teenagers, it was their first ever job and they learned a lot. Of course, it started with how to be a cabana boy, often through on-the-job training from those who were older and longer-tenured. But a larger part was learning how to treat customers, how to engage and respect them and meet their needs – especially when working on gratuities.

Some also fostered their entrepreneurial skills at the Palms. Take Brian Lawrence, one of the many friends of my dad who was a cabana boy in the mid-1970s. He found that the most annoying part of the job was bringing out the chairs, day in and day out. So he recruited his younger cousin to take on that task, and would throw the kid a few dollars out of his weekly tips. Grandpa Bob was not happy when he got wind, and yelled at Brian to stop subcontracting. But Brian would still sneak his cousin's help sometimes, willing to risk Grandpa's wrath, and gained a new business skill that he took with him into adulthood – the art of the subcontracting. Then there was Anthony Scire – now known as Z100 radio personality "Skeery Jones" – whose family belonged to the club in the 1980s. By this time, there were no longer official "deck boys" (it wasn't an enticing enough job description), and members without cabanas would have to grab a heavy mat out of the sweaty storage room and drag it themselves to a lounge chair. Anthony, only thirteen at the time, saw an opening in the job market. He created the unofficial "mat boy" job for himself, taking his place next to the mat room each morning. When members came by, he would energetically grab the mats, carry them out to the designated chairs, and the members – assuming this was Bob-endorsed – would give him a small tip. The next summer, Anthony would take a real job behind the snack bar, but this was his industrious on-ramp to working at the Palms.

While much of the cabana boys' work centered on schlepping and fetching, perhaps their most important but unpaid role was as eye candy. Along with the lifeguards, the cabana boys were the object of innocent summer crushes for the pre-teen and teenage girls who came with their families, as well as the young moms and middle-aged women and even grandmothers who spent their days at the Palms, while their husbands were at work. It was practically part of their daily routine – watching over the rims of their sunglasses, fawning and flirting, and for the younger girls, even trailing after the cute cabana boys. Picture Matt Dillon in *The Flamingo Kid*, constantly fending off passes made by women of all ages. For the most part, the cabana boys disregarded the attention as they went about their chores, though perhaps didn't hate being the eye candy (especially when it translated into extra tips). And as happens among any group thrown together day after day in the hot summer sun, teenage crushes often blossomed into something more. Many cabana boys had a summer fling—and some of those fleeting romances turned into lasting love stories. One such couple was Steve Finkelstein, a late-1960s cabana boy, and Shelley Blaustein, a teenage member spending the season with her family; what began as a summer romance grew into a lifelong partnership, now nearly fifty years and counting.

On rainy days, the cabana boys practically had the place to themselves – other than the most die-hard members, who showed up religiously, rain-or-shine, to play cards. They would run in the rain to fetch their food from the snack bar, but otherwise would hide out and themselves play poker or gin rummy. It was a learning experience for many —a first hands-on exposure to gambling—and some took to it more than others. Eric Yorke, a cabana boy in the 1970s, remembers tentatively joining his first such game and getting quickly trounced. He was just handing over his hard-earned money when my dad happened by. Ever protective, though himself just a teenager, my dad demanded the other cabana boys give Eric his money back – and instructed Eric to never play cards again. He may already have been a gambling savant by that age, a trait inherited from Grandpa Bob, but he knew it wasn't for everybody.

My dad was not the only one to get upset about rainy day shenanigans. One dreary day in the late 1970s, when my Uncle Larry and his cousin Philip were on cabana boy duty, the card players arrived and made their way to the Luau Room, at the time a popular rain refuge. But the door was locked. Another of the cabana boys, instead of helpfully tracking down the keys, told the members just to go home. Grandpa Bob, blaming his son and nephew for this poor customer management, let them have it. But it was perhaps nothing compared to one Sunday a few years earlier. It was pouring, and Brian Lawrence and a few other cabana boys confidently snuck out to the race track; they didn't expect the sun to come out so suddenly, and by the time they made their way back to the Palms, the members had already been streaming in. Needless to say, Grandpa Bob was not happy when his cabana boys were nowhere to be found, and made his feelings known.

The punishment for misbehavior from Grandpa Bob was usually the yelling – pretty impressive in itself. Sometimes it was an in-the-moment firing, and then a relenting the next day. But regular disrespect was not going to be tolerated. There was a showdown with one such cabana boy, Dirk, in the 1970s, who got under Grandpa's skin one too many times. Not playing around, Grandpa Bob yelled at him "The staff don't like you, the customers don't like you, I don't like you. Do us all a favor, and get out of here!" The teenager wasn't seen again.

Yes despite – or perhaps partly because of – his temper, Grandpa Bob was able to foster a real sense of camaraderie among the cabana boys. Of course, there was the competing and teasing and hazing among the boys. There were different personality types, so not everyone fully got along. But it was a bonding experience. They worked together, helped each other, joked around, vented their frustrations about the cabana members and Grandpa Bob.

From early morning cabana set-ups to after-hour shenanigans, a cabana boys' summer was a fully Palms experience – and for many, it was among the most memorable of their lives. They made solid money to cover the costs of college, they got to hang outside and spend time with friends, and – from working with Grandpa Bob and the cast of characters that frequented the Palms – they learned a lot. Perhaps more than any other job, the Palms was an education in hard work, responsibility, and people management. Many went on to become doctors, dentists and lawyers – in Brooklyn and beyond – with the Palms a solid foundation for their successful careers.

The Pools:
The Splashy Center of Action

Most of my memories of the Palms centered around the pools. I would spend the day playing games with my cousins, or trying to show off my newfound swimming skills. The big windows of the event hall overlooked the pool, and my older sister Jackie and I could look up and wave to my dad when he took a break from preparing for the evening's party. I envied Jackie and the other older kids, jumping and flipping off the two diving boards into the deep pool on the upper deck. So it was a big deal the day my eight-year-old self was first allowed to climb the steep ladder to the ten-foot diving board. Sun glaring, I glanced at my mom and at my favorite lifeguard Rory, who had known me since I was a baby, heard the calls of encouragement, and timidly hopped off the end of the plank, relishing the splash and letting myself be enveloped not only by the water but by the true spirit of summer.

The construction of the Palms Shore Club – and thereafter all of the activities and action – centered around the two enormous, glimmering blue rectangles. There was the main pool on the lower deck, a fifty-meter expanse where toddlers would splash around, where kids would take swimming lessons and play games,

Hanging by the pools in the 1960s (courtesy of Jennifer Proctor Simon)

My sister Jackie jumping off of the lower diving board in the 1990s, with my grandparents' house in the background

where middle-aged women in bikinis would take off their high heels temporarily to dip their toes while chatting, avoiding getting their perfectly-coiffed hair wet. Some of the older members would do lazy laps, one infamously swimming just once across the expanse each Sunday, arms raised above the water holding a razor and shaving cream, as a shortcut from the locker room to his cabana. Most of the older crowd rarely went in, only venturing into the main pool as a quick cool down during table game breaks. The joke was that one could tell how hot the day was by how many of the seniors made their way into the pool.

Then there was the diving pool on the adjacent upper deck, a fourteen-foot-deep fun zone for the Palms youth. For pre-teens to take hesitant jumps off of the imposing diving board or scream down a slide in the early days; for teenage boys to flip off of the lower diving board, showing off for the girls; for games of water polo or Marco Polo. For races, young members and staff alike would line up along the pool's edge and, at the word "go," dive to collect as many coins as they could from the rolls tossed to the bottom by the head lifeguard. The occasional rebellious teenager would get expelled from the pool area by the lifeguards for jumping over the fence at the edge of the diving pool, into the main pool below. Their friends would often be hanging out around the pool deck, lounging, flirting, laughing at any of the mishaps or reprimands.

Even when the pools were closed for the day, and the lifeguards stepped down from their posts, the bright blue expanses served as a backdrop to many a lovely summer evening. There were, of course, the popular Wednesday Night Dinners. Cocktail hours for big weddings or other events were also hosted in this central area, with arranged lounge chairs often serving as a visual—but precarious— boundary between the guests and the deep water. Some evenings, strong winds would blow food or paper goods into the water—just part of the charm.

The pools were a source of pride for Grandpa Bob, and he was eager to offer them up for local events, particularly in the Palms' first few years. In the summer of 1962, this included an aquatic show and swimming competition with Buster Crabbe, the two-time Olympic

Director Marilyn Marchs has the 8 - 12 year-old boys lined up for a swimming race.

Kids lined up for a swimming race in 1965, as captured in the Palms Shore Tattler

The Pools: The Splashy Center of Action

View of the waterfall edge between the two pools (courtesy of Paul Rosenblit)

medalist swimmer, and film and television actor – a memorable day for the winners, like ten-year-old Ricki Krauss, who were handed a trophy by the star.

As the pools were a centerpiece of the Palms experience, Grandpa Bob had very high standards for their maintenance. The head lifeguard was the one tasked with preserving the crystal-clear water and operating the impressive filter system throughout the summer. He would make his way into the dark, dank room under the pool deck where the massive filter system was housed, eyes tearing from chlorine fumes as he opened and closed the system each day. And under Grandpa Bob's watchful eye, he would supervise the lifeguard crew for above-ground maintenance, from scrubbing the decks to vacuuming the pool.

In the 1960s, Don G served as head lifeguard, before apparently moving on to become manager at the newly opened Roll-n-Roaster just down the block. After Don came Lou G, who stepped into the role and carried the torch for a time. By the 1970s, Steven G had taken over. Tall, athletic, and blonde, he earned the nickname "King of the Pools." He drew plenty of attention — especially from the ladies — even with his ever-present and not-so-sexy nose clips. But Steven had no time for joking or flirting. He ran a tight ship, keeping the rowdy teenagers in line and doing his best to uphold Grandpa Bob's famously high standards.

Of course, there were still the occasional slip-ups. Like the time two lifeguards, Steven's younger brother Burt and Richie S, got a little too enthusiastic with the soap on the pool deck carpet. The sea of bubbles they created drifted into the diving pool and down into the locker rooms below — and naturally, bubbled up Grandpa Bob's ire in the process.

Despite that incident, Burt, who was best known for his hot pink speedo, eventually took over as head lifeguard himself. He carried forward the lessons he'd learned (sometimes the hard way) and passed them on to Paul Rosenblit, who passed them on again. And so it went, one head lifeguard after another, each shaped by the stories, the stumbles, and the high standards passed down through the years.

The upper pool deck set up for a lovely evening cocktail hour

The Pools: The Splashy Center of Action

Highlight in the Brooklyn Daily in Aug 1962 about aquatic show and swimming competition with Olympian Buster Crabbe

The lifeguards had their hands full. Keeping the pools clean kept them busy, and sometimes that meant facing the unexpected. Like the time Randy Gottlieb, a lifeguard in the 1970s, had to fish a live eel out of the pool after a passing seagull dropped it in mid-flight. Then there was also the daily routine: yelling and blowing whistles at kids of all ages to stop running, stop hanging on the ropes, stop trying ridiculous stunts off the diving boards. And when warnings didn't work, the lifeguards had to kick troublemakers out of the pool — most often young teenagers, who took it as a challenge. Steven, in particular, seemed to relish that part of the job.

Then there were the injuries the lifeguards had to handle, the cuts and bruises that often resulted when their warnings weren't heeded— kids who ran into the lifeguard chairs, or were bleeding from a fall on the concrete. In the 1970s, my dad's cousin Melissa, while learning to dive, made one attempt too close to the edge of the pool and came up bleeding. Everyone came running, as an injury to the Berfond baby was simply unacceptable. David Schub remembers when he was eleven-years old, trying to show off his ability to swim underwater the full length of the olympic-sized pool during peak swimming hours – and getting accidentally kicked in the eye. It was bad enough to require a doctor's visit. Another time, a little boy decided to jump into the pool backwards, catching his chin on the side and actually requiring an ambulance to come and stitch it up. There were also the occasional water-related incidents that required the lifeguards to dive in, for instance to scoop up little kids whose parents were too distracted by conversations with their friends. Longtime lifeguard Rory Staines remembers diving in to save a three-year-old boy named Rob Garguilo, who had confidently ridden his Big Wheel plastic tricycle straight into the water.

Perhaps a less official role for the lifeguards, as well as the cabana boys, was to be the subject of admiration for young cabana club members – both the all-male lifeguard crews in the 60s and 70s, and the more female, bikini-clad crews of the 80s and 90s, under the

Water polo games in the diving pool

leadership of head lifeguards like Jennifer K and Jeanmarie Staines. Idolization, crushes, you name it.

Steven G played another role during his tenure: coach and organizer of the water polo team. For many years, the Palms Shore Club young men and women boasted surprisingly strong water polo skills. Sometimes there were friendly games within the Palms family, lifeguards against cabana boys. But particularly in the 1970s, the young men and women from the Palms excelled in playing against teams from other cabana clubs in the Brooklyn area – the El Caribe, the Deauville, Silver Gull. The Palms diving pool, deep all around, was the best set-up for matches, with longtime and well-liked member Al Pantoch acting as the official – though voluntary – referee while his children David and Allison played. David was part of the all-star men's team, along with other members like John G and Arthur G (affectionately known as "Tarzan" for his size and strength), as well as some of the lifeguards. On Thursday evenings, there would be hundreds of people watching – around the pool, from their cabanas, wherever they could, cheering the players on, most often to a Palms victory.

Beyond games, the centrality of the pools made them a location for many youth pranks. One day, cabana boy John M decided to prove he could jump off the high diving board while *in* a folding chair. Another time, on a Wednesday evening after a few drinks, cabana boy Jeff Douglas and Aidan, an Irish exchange student, decided to toss some furniture *into* the diving pool, fully submerging them. A table and chairs stood fully upright at the bottom of the fourteen-feet deep pool, and had to be fished out by Burt G the next morning, entertainment for the lifeguards and members alike.

The Snack Bar: A Moving Heart

I can still smell the wafting scent of French fries, even over the smell of chlorine when I walked into the snack bar, an oversized t-shirt thrown on over my bathing suit after a few hours in the pool. Still dripping wet, I would confidently step up to the counter to order: most often a hot dog or chicken tenders alongside my favorite steak fries. Willie and the guys behind the counter knew me and were always overly generous. While I generally knew my way around the whole Palms Shore Club, the 1990s deli location was right in the center of my most comfortable domain: stretching between Grandpa Bob's store and Grandma Gloria's newer office and leading out to the cabanas that our family tended to overtake. It was bright, and clean, and I could order whatever I wanted, when I wanted it – a little kid's dream. I'd grab my plastic tray tightly, and like so many before me, take my feast to wherever my heart desired.

The snack bar was the heart of the Palms Shore Club from the day it opened. It had many incarnations over the years, moving locations at least four times in as many decades, based on what seemed to be somewhat arbitrary decision-making of Grandpa Bob – a running joke for regulars at the club.

But no matter its location, from 1962 on, the snack bar was the busiest and most hectic area of the Palms. Serving up delicious food all day long, and anchoring countless memories. Cabana boys came and went, commandeering the place as they placed and picked up orders for the members in their cabana rows, joking or arguing with whoever was behind the counter or at the cash register. If the snack bar was the heart of the Palms, the cabana boys were the veins. The cashier would keep tabs of how much the cabana boys ordered and owed – and at the end of the day, they would settle up. Cindy Solomon, who worked the register in the 1970s among her many gigs at Palms, remembers the enormous piece of paper on which she'd manually tally the orders in columns and rows, Grandpa

Bob breathing down her neck to ensure she captured everything on each tray.

Tabs would add up quickly throughout the day: For breakfast, bagels with *shmear* or bacon and egg sandwiches (or even bagels with bacon *and* cream cheese). For lunch, hamburgers or grilled cheese (with tomato or bacon); tuna salad or corned beef or pastrami sandwiches. For the ladies on a 'diet', maybe half a cantaloupe with a ton of cottage cheese plopped in the center or a salad with an accompanying malt. Egg creams or ice cream cones for mid-day snacks. Coffees, and iced coffees and more coffees, at all hours.

Fresh bread and desserts were baked daily on premises for many years. In the sixties and seventies, when the snack bar was located in the first floor of the building, there was an adjacent small kitchen dedicated for the baker nestled against a hip-height storage closet known as Cousin Itt's room. Trays with Danishes, cookies, rolls and other fresh baked goods would be laid out, their delicious aromas wafting into the hallway, tempting the cabana boys into quick snack raids while making their rounds.

On weekends, there were competing mouthwatering smells of Italian cooking – meatball heroes and gravy and other specialties whipped up by Larry Genovese, another Palms Shore Club lifer, often with a kid like Alan Horowitz or Philip G assisting under his tutelage. Along with his famous antipasti salad, the dishes would be available to members as part of the snack bar offerings.

Good food was key to keeping members purchasing on site, and Grandpa Bob knew it. Outside food and drinks were permitted (reluctantly), but not in the snack bar itself, one of Grandpa Bob's strict rules. The sandwiches from the deli across Emmons Avenue – first Patsy's and then Noel's – were neighborhood favorites among members and staff alike; but those Italian heroes and roast beef sandwiches better be eaten far from sight. Grandpa Bob was not shy about berating anyone who broke that rule, or who tried to grab plastic utensils or condiments without buying food. He would yell at them until they slunk back empty-handed.

While some cost-conscious members dragged coolers of homemade food into the cabanas—one family even sneaking in a mini refrigerator—many couldn't resist the snack bar's temptations, ensuring a steady business.

Many adults loved nothing more than to accompany their tasty Palms meal with a refreshing alcoholic beverage – and Grandpa Bob was not going to miss out. The Palms did have an outdoor bar on the back deck that was open all-day on the weekends and for the famous adults-only Wednesday night dinners. While many members did bring their own liquor, there was a regular crew who were happy to splurge on screwdrivers or spritzes, whiskey sours or sea breezes. They'd start tabs or pay cash into the infamously low-tech cashier system –a tin box. Teenagers would also sidle up to the bar, ordering mocktails like a virgin strawberry daiquiri or pina colada.

Working at the snack bar or drinks bar was a common gig for many in the Berfond extended family. In the 1960s, when the snack bar was located in the sweltering first floor of the building, at the helm was Grandma Gloria's mother, my Great Grandmother, Sadie Heiser. Kind, but keen and no nonsense, she worked the cash register – and did her best to keep the scheming cabana boys in line. Especially when it came to the tomatoes. Tomatoes were considered extra on sandwiches, an additional 15 or 20 cents. The ever-industrious Palms cabana boys like Barry Weinstein had learned – and passed on to each other – that they could pocket the extra money if they didn't share with the cashier that the sandwiches had tomatoes when they read out their orders, but charged the members for it anyway. Sadie learned to ask explicitly about tomatoes, and when the answer was consistently 'no', she began to inspect every sandwich herself. She was tough, an inspector general. (But she had a soft side, too: between the rushes, she would sew beautiful custom Barbie Doll clothes that teenage staff bought as gifts for their younger sisters.)

Over the years, Grandma Sadie stepped away, and many took their turns at the snack bar—working the cash register, manning the grill or sandwich counter, pouring the coffee, or restocking paper goods. The crew learned to be fast and efficient, especially during the lunchtime rush. They memorized orders, mastered multitasking, and always prioritized the cabana boys. Willie S, the "King of the Counter" for many years, whipped up the best bacon, egg and cheese sandwiches or deli subs with ease – even when bombarded with custom requests. While they worked hard, it was generally a good gig, and in the downtime, the team could joke around and have fun. Cary M, who worked there in the 1970s, perfected his impersonation of Grandpa Bob, a crowd favorite – alongside his celebrated caricature of Bob. Others might start mild food fights during slow periods, catching their buddies off guard with tossed slices of deli meat. A few would sneak off to the refrigerators for a high from the pressurized Reddi-Whip cans.

Yet, given its centrality, the snack bar could be the most stressful place to work. Members always wanted more: when their ice cream was being scooped, "put more muscle into it!". When their sandwich meats were being sliced, "keep going, pile it high!". Older women would squirrel away extras or return food with complaints: the toast is too burned! There is too much milk in the coffee! Grandpa Bob might have to arbitrate, assessing whether a refund was warranted. The cabana boys bore the brunt of the chaos, sprinting back and forth between the snack bar and cabanas, sweating to achieve the elusive perfection for their customers.

And then there was Grandpa Bob himself. The snack bar was always under his domain, and whenever he was around, the whole vibe changed. He managed the staff closely, his sharp eye missing nothing. Sometimes, that wasn't so bad. His little cousin, Andy Berfond, worked at the coffee station in the early 1960s, when the snack bar briefly operated next to the bar on the second floor. At fourteen, he couldn't quite reach the towering coffee urns for refills, so Grandpa Bob had the floor raised to make the job possible.

But Grandpa Bob's high standards, low tolerance, and quick temper came down hard on several staff members over the years. Including his own sons. In the late 1970s, my Uncle Mel was working the snack bar, while also pitching in to work the back bar upstairs. Uncle Mel was finishing up there one Sunday evening when he heard his father scream his name over the intercom, the whole place listening. Over the phone, Grandpa Bob demanded that Uncle Mel come down to meet him in the snack bar. Weary and sweaty from an endless weekend, Uncle Mel trudged down the two flights of stairs to the brutally hot room. Grandpa was furious that the protective glass windows at the snack bar – Uncle Mel's responsibility! – looked filthy, and despite his son's long hours, forced him to wash the glass right then and there.

Grandpa Bob's meticulous oversight of the snack bar never changed. Under his piercing blue eyes, every surface had to be cleaned the right way, spotless, every day – the equipment had to be taken apart and wiped down, pots and pans scrubbed, often by the teenagers at the bottom of the staff totem pole. The snack bar staff didn't work off tips like the cabana boys— except for end-of-summer contributions from the more generous members. But if you dared to ask about a raise for the long and sometimes grueling hours, Grandpa Bob was most likely to respond with, "I'll give you a raise—a raise through the roof."

In addition to cleanliness, Grandpa Bob was hyper-attuned to stealing and waste. In the 1970s, Uncle Mel was working the grill while a guy named Manny was in charge of sandwiches. He was, in Uncle Mel's memory, a real sandwich artist, with his own set of professional knives. But the ever-watchful Grandpa Bob suspected Manny of stealing the tuna fish cans – and put Uncle Mel on the case to monitor him. Begrudgingly, Uncle Mel kept an eye on Manny, and sure enough, saw him pocketing several small tin cans. When Uncle Mel told his dad, Grandpa Bob chased Manny out to the street, and no one ever saw the sandwich artist again. Uncle Mel became the new sandwich master.

One day in the 1980s, Jonathan R was trying to get ahead of the Sunday lunch rush and put a few dozen burgers and hot dogs on the grill. Yet, just as he was starting to pull them off, the sky turned dark and the clouds opened, rain pouring down. There would be no rush now, as the Palms turned into a ghost town in the rain. Grandpa Bob walked into the snack bar, his face turning purple as he registered the fresh-grilled meat as money down the drain. Poor Jonathan was subject to a rant, including a few choice words, with my grandpa's legitimate complaint about not wanting to waste food coming out in stereotypical Bob fashion.

My mom, Barbie, working with her best friend Barbara Reich Borrero at the outdoor bar in the late 1970s

Though perhaps no one bore the brunt of Grandpa Bob's yelling more than teenager Anthony Scire. Anthony would keep his head down, scrubbing grease off pots or pouring coffee, as Grandpa Bob let off steam, sometimes for mistakes, and sometimes for no reason at all.

Working at the outdoor drinks bar was certainly a more easy-going and lucrative gig. During the weekend, the bar was a destination for the "Good Time Charlie" types – the (real and perceived) Palms big-shots who liked to drink and joke around and spend money. They would finish their card games and spend hours at the bar – meandering from one vice to another – cigars hanging out of their mouths the whole time. Two popular guests, Tony Z and Marvin Urban, would often buy rounds of drinks for everyone, racking up bills of several hundred dollars. The pair generously tipped the young women bartending—which in the late '70s and early '80s, often included my mom, Barbie, alongside her friends Barbara Reich Borrero or Rita Kirschenbaum Kestenbaum. Tony in particular was known for being one of the Palms' best tippers, and the bar was where his generosity shone.

Bartending was also a front-seat to some of the Palms Shore Club drama. Letitia Yemma, who worked there in the mid-80s, remembers an affair between two cabana club members that centered around the outdoor bar. The man and woman would regularly meet up there, have a drink together – and jump apart if the wife happened to stroll by. Except one night, when it all came to a head. Perhaps the cheating couple didn't separate quickly enough. The two women ended up going at it, fists flying, until some of the men nearby stepped in. Needless to say, the affair was no longer secret after that.

Even as the outdoor bar generated its share of stories, Grandpa Bob's attention always circled back to the snack bar—his pride and joy. He always made sure the snack bar was on top of the trends. When the New York-based Snapple company started broadly selling beverages in the early eighties, he was quick to jump on the bandwagon. The Palms became a "Snapple House." Then came the FrozFruit craze. For a few summers, teenagers flocked to the snack bar, forsaking plain ice cream for ice pops studded with chunks of real fruit. Though marketed as a healthier option, and often dismissed as less indulgent, Grandpa Bob understood the appeal. The FrozFruit bars regularly sold out.

The Snack Bar in its fourth incarnation in the late 1980s, at the Marina, overlooking the Bay

Uncle Larry, who regularly worked the snack bar over the years, attempted a few innovations of his own in his father's footsteps. He once tried to institute a receipt system to replace the tried-and-true method of calling out orders, a well-intentioned but overcomplicated update that was abandoned within a week. It didn't take much to keep the snack bar what it was: the pulsing heart that nourished the Palms Shore Club's summer community.

As the decades passed, the snack bar continued to evolve, following Grandpa Bob's ever-restless vision. In the late eighties, when the marina was built out on the Bay, Grandpa Bob decided to move the snack bar there so people could dock their boats and come in for lunch or a snack. Time and money were invested, and the members enjoyed the new setting, but the expected revenue from outside customers never came. After just a few summers, another move was underway.

By the early nineties, a new location had been identified—right at the front of the Palms. Grandpa Bob removed a small row of low-demand cabanas, creating a larger space with an entrance from Emmons Avenue. Named the Palms Emporium, the snack bar morphed into a bodega-style store with a deli just behind it, open year-round to the Sheepshead Bay neighborhood. It was his baby, the place where Grandpa Bob could almost always be found, keeping his critical eye on everything while playing cards at one of the square tables nearby.

The Emporium represented the legacy of Grandpa Bob. Though the Palms was entering its final decade, his drive to reinvent never faded. He took pride in the idea that the Emporium extended the cabana club's spirit beyond the summer months, a place where locals could still gather, share stories, and feel part of something familiar. Even as the seasons changed and the sounds of splashing and laughter quieted, the heartbeat of the Palms lived on behind the deli counter.

Table Games: The Best Way to Spend A Summer Day

I remember the sly sense of satisfaction I felt when I'd lay the final card face-down on the pile and slowly spread my ten-card hand across the table. Gin! I did it, I'd earned one of Grandpa Bob's rare smiles, half-hidden beneath his dusty white moustache. Maybe he let me win, but my nine year old ego didn't notice – or maybe just didn't care. I loved those moments of his attention and pride, the small triumphs that came from mastering the gin-rummy skills that he - and my dad - gruffly but lovingly imparted. We'd often practice at his "throne," one of the square tables up front in the Palms store, when he wasn't playing for money. Only years later did I realize that our matches were part of a time-honored Palms tradition.

From the very first summer of the Palms Shore Club, adult members oriented their days around a few favorite table games: mahjong and canasta (with the occasional Rummikub) for the women, and gin-rummy and poker for the men. In the 1960s, there was even a whole area designated for cards on the back patio overlooking the Bay, before newer structures like the Luau Room and stage were built. It wasn't that the Palms lacked other entertainment, but in the hazy Brooklyn heat, these games made the long summer days fly by.

Throughout the week, groups of four women – and "Mahjong Marvin" – would sit for hours, gabbing and gossiping while keeping meticulous track of each other's points and wins. They took their games seriously, almost religiously, sometimes bickering over who owed who twenty-five cents. But mostly, it was just an enjoyable way to pass the time. They'd send cabana boys for snacks or coffees, wade into the pool to cool off between rounds, and occasionally glance toward their children, who played nearby or napped in strollers under the watchful eyes of teenage "mother's helpers" paid fifty cents an hour. For many women, a day at the Palms was

Table Games: The Best Way to Spend A Summer Day

beautifully predictable: rain or shine, they'd arrive, sit down at table, and play—wide-brimmed hats shading their faces, stylish sunglasses glinting, elastic bands keeping cards from flying away on windy afternoons. Only when the cabana boys came around at dusk to fold up the tables did they reluctantly pack up their belongings and call it a day. The men had their own rhythms, and their own tables. While some played gin-rummy, the real action was always at the four to five dedicated poker tables. Over the years, the location shifted, but the cast of card sharks remained the same: middle-aged and older men with cigars hanging loosely from their mouths, hats protecting their balding heads and shielding their eyes while their bare arms burned. Quietly serious, they would glare at each other, then their cards, casually toying with their piles of chips, barely speaking except to call, raise or fold.

A pleasant diversion for the ladies, as they enjoy the sun and relax at their favorite pastimes.

Ladies at play in the 1967 summer season, as captured in the Palms Shore Tattler

The Palms Shore Club

"The Supreme Court is now in session."

One or two lucky cabana boys would "run" these games, a coveted job with a lot of demands but also serious perks. It was one of my dad's first real jobs as a teenager at the Palms in the 1970s, paired up with his friends Ronald Kestenbaum, Alan Horowitz and Brian Lawrence. They'd set up the folding tables in the morning, lay out the cards and chips, and stay on call all day, making sure the players never had to get up or break their concentration. They fetched sandwiches and burgers from the snack bar, pitchers of cold water, cigars, cigarettes and alcoholic beverages. They kept the games stocked with fresh packs of Tally-Ho playing cards. By evening, they'd tally each player's tab, sometimes with a little rounding up, and collect their generous tips. The money these teenagers earned in a single summer could rival the best adult salaries in Brooklyn, and the rest of the young staff looked on in envy.

And then there was the Big Game—the table that drew the heaviest hitters and the highest stakes. Each weekend, in a scene worthy of a Scorsese film, the regulars would take their seats: Mel M, Hank

B, big Julie, Tony Z, Mike R, Frankie M, and others. They'd rib each other, light cigars, and buy in, their stacks of chips towering in front of them. Wives and friends gathered behind them, whispering and watching as "big money" changed hands. In the early years, Duke, a tall, bearded man with sun-worn skin, was one of the fixtures at that table. Duke owned a successful business and was generous with his winnings, lavishly tipping the cabana boys who ran the game – including his own son, Richie, for a few summers.

For the most part, the players in the Big Game were civil and polite, but sometimes tempers flared when big winnings were at stake. In the 1970s, Grandpa Bob moved the table to the roof of the newly-built Luau Room to limit the onlookers. But even seclusion couldn't dampen the ritual that carried on season after season, as much a part of Palms' DNA as the pool, the snack bar, and the summer sun.

Mahjoniks Incorporated . . . Palms favorite fraternity.

Members playing away the summer day – men at poker, women at Mahjong – as captured in the Palms Shore Tattler in 1964

The Palms Shore Club

Men and women enjoying the table games Labor Day 1987

Palms Shore Day Camp: Don't Forget the Kids

I was too young to be party to the tween drama, only four years old at the time. But the story and outrage persisted over the years, perhaps even growing in legend. My eleven-year-old cousin Jenine, Uncle Larry's oldest daughter, was devastated. The injustice! While she didn't go regularly to the camp, given the longer commute from her family's house in New Jersey, she had her heart set on the role of Ariel in The Little Mermaid, the 1992 selection for the important Palms Day Camp end-of-summer production. She had starred in family performances and was destined for greatness. But our grandparents wouldn't even let her try out for one of the lead roles. She was relegated to the chorus, just like her little sister Nicole, while her crushes and frenemies were cast as leads – Lonny Friedland as Sebastian and Peri Anderson as Ariel. It was reverse nepotism! To this day, just a mention of The Little Mermaid to Jenine can spur intense feelings – just one example of how the Palms Day Camp could etch memories that lasted a lifetime.

My grandparents wanted the Palms Shore Club to be a holistic experience of summer fun. And for the adults to truly enjoy their days at the Palms – playing mahjong and poker, sunning and drinking – they needed some way to keep their children occupied. So began the Palms Shore Day Camp.

With so many amenities already available, the Camp did not need much. Grandpa Bob designated an area toward the back of the property, behind the sports courts, for the purpose. There was an old bungalow he had purchased, which they readily converted into a camp-house with tables, and then added a small concrete kiddie pool (unfortunately without a filter). To help keep the kiddos

The cast of the Camp's memorable 1992 show, The Little Mermaid, with their impressive costumes (courtesy of Hilarie Simon Gottlieb)

corralled, they also set up a gate and hired a 'guard' – like Bob "Rosey" Rosenblatt, in one of his many roles over the years.

Grandma Gloria hired a director and several teenage counselors, sourcing recruits from among the Palms member families and their broader network. And the rest of the members were more than happy to dispatch their children for the day, appreciating the option to keep their children close-by but not under-foot, supervised and occupied by others for several hours per day, six days per week (with Mondays off).

Despite seeming like a glorified babysitting service, there was a fairly classic camp set-up: children would be grouped by age, and be supervised by a pair of counselors through a relatively informal schedule of activities designated by the director—a role filled over the years by Elane, Nancy, Lois, Alison, and others. They kept the kids active with hopscotch and jump rope, paddleball and dodge-ball on the nearby courts, swimming in the large shallow pool, or splashing around in the kiddie pool. As a reprieve from the heat, there were plenty of arts-and-crafts options, painting, popsicle-stick constructions, lanyard-making, and more. They'd break for lunchtime and snack time, which often included a vat of the infamous "bug juice," a bright red, fruit punch-adjacent concoction that one of the counselors would mix in the kitchen. Cindy Solomon, a counselor in the mid 1970s, remembers Grandpa Bob stopping by to drop off the snacks or quietly just check-in; little kids were a secret soft-spot for him.

On rainy days, the groups would all come together in the camp house, watching movies

The young performers being directed in Camp 'Sing' in 1976 (courtesy of Eddie Reavan)

and engaging in tamer activities – a favorite setup for the teenage counselors, who got to hang with their friends and flirt with their crushes. Cousin "Big Larry" Berfond remembers setting up a projector for these movie days, in the pre-television era.

There was also Color War to channel the kids' competitive spirit, and the occasional exciting field trip—perhaps to Adventureland, the amusement park in Farmingdale, about an hour's drive away on Long Island. And at the end of summer came the all-important camp show for the rest of the members. Some years, a specific musical – *Annie, Peter Pan,* of course, *The Little Mermaid*. Other years it took the form of a thematic production, like the *"Salute to Walt Disney"* in 1989, or the *"Salute to Music"* dance show in 1995. With the support of other members, costumes were sewn, scenery painted, and the campers energetically (if not skillfully) rehearsed for the big performance.

The Palms Shore Club

The dance moves of campers in the 1988 show, featuring my four-year-old sister Jackie first on the left

The Camp wasn't without its chaos. The cubby area, meant to be an orderly space where campers could stash their towels and extra clothes or discreetly change out of wet bathing suits, often transformed into a humid jungle of belongings and shrieking, half-dressed children. Counselors tried valiantly to maintain order, but it was often a losing battle. Some of the more restless campers would make daring escapes, sneaking through the gate toward their parents on the other side of the club. Like Abbe Elrich Poznak, whose father, Julie, was a well-respected maître d' of the nightclub upstairs. Inevitably, the runaways were corralled and coaxed back through the gate, usually laughing the whole way.

Of course, with dozens of kids swarming the camp area every day, injuries were inevitable. In the 1980s, accident-prone camper David Schub remembers slamming face-first into a gatepost while trying to make a catch during stickball, earning himself an emergency trip to the dentist. Another camper barely survived his counselor's aim—Will Greenhut nearly flattened a kid during a particularly intense dodgeball game. And in one notable reversal, a sweet-faced four-year-old unleashed a flurry of punches on his counselor, fifteen-year-old Lonny Friedland, after being told to sit still, continuing the assault even after Lonny marched him outside the gate to his mother and grandmother.

Many of the Berfond family passed through the camp, whether as campers or in the annual shows. My dad went in the 1960s, before he was passably old enough to work at the Palms. Eight-year-old Allen appeared in *Peter Pan* alongside his friends, including Alan Horowitz, who played Captain Hook. His brothers, Larry and Mel, also attended the camp, and years later, my sister and cousins took their own turns in the legendary end-of-summer camp productions.

Family involvement didn't end there. My dad's cousin, Arlyn Brenner, Aunt Sheila's daughter, attended camp as a child and later became a counselor in the late 1960s. She and their second cousin Larry Berfond also handled camp transportation, a service offered as part of the day camp fees for parents who weren't at the club daily. Each morning, Arlyn and Larry would drive the family's old burgundy station wagon around Sheepshead Bay, picking up kids and making pit stops at Nathan's Famous for French fries to fuel their day—a smell that lingered in the car (and on the campers) for hours. By late afternoon, the kids who weren't driven home would rejoin their families in the main part of the club – often diving straight into the pool, loud and laughing, marking their presence and the joyful close of another Palms Shore summer day.

The Switchboard: A Summer Soundtrack

I remember a sense of tranquility during my summer days at the Palms. Yes, there was a steady strum of summer sounds – the low sounds of members' radios, kids splashing in the pool, members laughing over their card games – but it all melded together into a comforting and happy hum of the cabana club community. I could climb up to an empty terrace or sneak off to an empty paddleball court, the next Sweet Valley Twins installment at hand, and know that I wouldn't be interrupted or overwhelmed by loud stereo-ed voices or music. I had no idea that this wasn't always the case — that in the first half of its lifetime, the Palms cabana club had a very specific and memorable summer soundtrack of its own.

"Beverly November, telephone call for Beverly November." Well before the era of smartphones and other personal devices, the only thing that could interrupt the easy rhythm of summer sounds was the Palms' public announcement system. Aside from the daily 'no call announcements' break from 1-3pm, names would blare through the overhead speakers all day, echoing throughout the club—the only distraction that prompted members to pause their mahjong or gin-rummy games and see if someone might be looking for them. Most often, it was the same few members being paged—creating local celebrities of the loudspeaker, known just from having their names constantly echoing across the grounds. Some even joked these women orchestrated calls just to keep their names in rotation. Beverly November, of course; but also Linda Witz and Sheila Cohen, all dedicated, daily Palms-goers.

Sheila Cohen was once in the pool when she was paged, and as she jumped out, dripping wet, to answer the phone, an electric shock sent her flying—a memorable incident for poor Sheila, but it didn't stop the endless stream of calls for her and the others.

And it wasn't just members receiving incoming calls from beyond the Palms gates. Sometimes it was staff being tracked down in the large complex ("Seymour, to the snack bar!"). Other times, it was staff or members amusing themselves with pranks, paging someone "to the bottom of the pool." Teenage girls called for the boys they liked and hung up as soon as they answered.

Behind these alerts were the switchboard operators, a few young women Grandma Gloria hired to take shifts in the tiny, dimly lit room near the Palms entrance, answering and directing the calls that came in through the dedicated switchboard system. My dad's cousin Arlyn, who helped with the switchboards in the mid-1970's – just one of her many jobs – remembered feeling like Lily Tomlin, who often played a telephone switchboard operator on the sketch comedy show

The Palms switchboard operators identified with Lily Tomlin's character Ernestine on Rowan & Martin's Laugh-In (1969-1973)

Laugh-In. Headphones on, moving plugs and flipping switches as the lights blinked across the ten stations, she did her best to maintain a calm, pleasant tone even in the midst of chaos.

Wednesdays were the busiest days for the switchboard operators, as members would call nonstop wanting to find out what was on the menu for the famous Wednesday night dinner. The answer mattered; it often determined whether they'd come in that evening. My mother's best friend, Barbara Reich Borrero, remembered how she and the others would answer the calls, with an exhausting but amusing refrain:

"Palms, can I help you? Chicken.
Palms, can I help you? Chicken.
Palms, can I help you?..."

While it could certainly be repetitive, it was considered a great job. The environment was casual, and between calls, the women could joke and have fun, smoking cigarettes when they pleased, even in the stifling, windowless room. Susan Fagen Britt, an operator in the 1960s, made up special names for members who preferred not to have their real ones announced over the PA system. Dory Chasanoff, who worked in the 1970s along with Rona Halbreich and Marjorie, remembered inventing names just to see who was paying attention.

They'd let some of the younger kids come into the room to "help" with the switchboard—really, to play with the cords and plugs they found so fascinating. Others would stop by to take a turn at the board or just hang out with the cute switchboard girls. That easy access sometimes came at a price: one day, an unknown culprit poured liquid all over the back of the system, and Susan Fagen Britt recalled the chaos when the power was turned on—the lights flickering like a Christmas tree, calls abruptly dropping, and the girls scrambling to keep their distance until the damage could be repaired.

By the 1980s, the switchboard and PA system were phased out. Not only had the technology become outdated, but the constant paging had turned into a nuisance for many, interrupting the otherwise tranquil atmosphere. A few pay phones were installed around the club instead, and staff could track down members in person, if emergency calls came in.

Like so much else at the Palms Shore Club, the switchboard became a fond relic of a different era—one more layer in the vivid, sometimes chaotic, always unforgettable soundscape of summers past.

Wednesday Night Dinners: A Timeless Tradition with Offshoots

When I close my eyes, I can quickly bring myself back to the hot, lazy Wednesday evenings. I am sitting next to my grandma at a folding table, as she punches holes on the members' cards, making sure they only make their way through the line once. If I breathe in, I can smell the smoke and aromas wafting over to us from the long buffet tables; pans and platters brimming with delicious food, an enticing display. I see my dad and the cabana boys all lined up behind the tables, serving tools in hand, appearing like an armed guard, a well-oiled machine, ready to portion out the contents to the over-eager patrons; Uncle Larry stationed at the BBQ pit, to serve the chicken and burgers; my sister Jackie or older cousins, Nicole and Jenine, perhaps helping to hand out plastic utensils. All hands were on deck—literally. I can still feel the buzz that filled the air on those summer evenings.

The infamous Wednesday Night Dinners were a hallmark of the Palms Shore Club summer season, a staple from its 1962 opening to the very end. No matter who you ask, those evenings of food and entertainment remain among the fondest memories.

This was the only weeknight when the Palms was open late, but it was adults only – young children were sent home, and the older ones were sent to fend for themselves at other restaurants on the block. Some tried to stick around, hiding in cabanas and attempting to sneak plates of food, but if they got caught, they were subject to Grandpa Bob's wrath. Most of the adults were happy with the child-free vibe: they had a carefree evening to enjoy a "free" meal and entertainment. Nothing could animate the middle-aged and older Brooklynites more.

They would line up hours in advance, dragging their chairs over to sit and gossip until dinner opened at 5 pm, hoping to be the first

Members lined up excitedly for Wednesday Night dinners in 1967, as captured in the Palms Shore Tattler

to get their pick. The tables of food were arranged alongside the diving pool. On windy evenings, there was always the risk of food blowing into the pool—but the event went on anyway: it was a risk worth taking. The set-up was intentional as it created a natural mechanism for forcing the hordes of hungry members into manageable lines. Every member was allowed through the line only once, and Grandma Gloria enforced it by punching their cards for that week. Many tried to weasel around the system: some had excuses for not having their cards with them or why the hole was already punched; others tried to sneak into the line to fill an additional plate for their kids stowed away in cabanas or guests that slipped in to partake in the free meal. But most ended up getting caught; Grandma was a bit too shrewd.

With their pass punched, members would make their way down the line, doing whatever they could to heap on the servings, regularly begging for more, for another scoop – ultimately needing two hands to balance the overloaded plates on their walk back. Grandpa Bob or another Berfond was always in charge of cutting or doling out the meat to limit serving size, with cabana boys or other staff in charge of the sides like potatoes, salads and rolls.

Everybody always wanted as much Palms food as they could get, eager for any free morsels they could squirrel away. Some older members, likely motivated by their Depression-era youth, would hoard what they could from the snack bar during the day, stocking their winter supplies of jam packets and Sweet'N'Low. But nothing could compare to the fervor of Wednesday Night Dinners. Some came armed with aluminum foil to wrap any bread or leftovers to bring home.

Long lines for Wednesday Night Dinners continued throughout the years, captured here in July 1981

Wednesday Night Dinners: A Timeless Tradition with Offshoots

Grandpa Bob and my dad Allen preparing heaping plates for members at a Wednesday Night Dinner in the late 1960s

The selection was a rotating cast of favorites, often part of themed offerings – the classic American BBQ nights with burgers and barbecued chicken; Italian nights with eggplant rollatini and linguini & broccoli; the surprisingly popular Chinese nights, with lo mein, egg rolls and sweet & sour chicken. In the early years, a lucky child – like my Uncle Larry when he was five or six years old in the 1960s – would wear a sandwich board with the menu options, forced to adorably march around the rows of cabanas.

Of course, for an adults-only evening, the drinks really flowed. The outdoor bar would be at its busiest, especially on the rare special occasion when bartenders handed out complimentary glasses of wine. One night, Jeanmarie Staines was bartending when they actually ran out of wine. She sent her sister Rory to ask for more from my dad, who was in charge at the time. Poor Rory did not expect the response she got when, tired from the long day, he screamed out "Squirrels! They're not getting anything else. Tell your sister, no more!"

Morty Gunty brought the house down when he entertained members at the Wednesday night Patio Party.

Comedian Morty Gunty performing at Wednesday Night Dinner in 1967, as captured in the Palms Shore Tattler

Shocked, Rory went back to her sister empty-handed. The members would have to make do with drink alternatives.

Despite such hiccups, the food and drinks were a tried-and-true formula for a successful evening. Yet Grandpa Bob still found ways to innovate. One early experiment: whole pigs on spits. It was one of the first few years the Palms was open, likely the mid-60s, when Grandpa Bob decided to set up two spits with roasting pigs, complete with apples in their mouths. What started as a good idea quickly turned into chaos, as members started pulling meat off of the spinning animals themselves, clearly tempted by the rich aromas and unwilling to wait for the staff to cut it off for them.

Grandma Gloria was both disgusted and furious – and the roasting pigs were no more.

But even without meat mayhem, it was never a boring evening. Members would take their heaping plates back to their cabanas or out by the stage; cabana boys – after helping out however was needed – would climb on the diving boards or other perch points (happy to relax before the nightmare of cleaning their rows after the late evening). All would settle in for an evening of entertainment.

Most of the time, it was PG-rated entertainment: comedians, singers, bands. Several Borscht Belt entertainers—stars of the lively Catskills resort scene that drew New York's Jewish vacationers in those years—made the rounds, including the talented songstress Joanne Engel, who was a regular. "The Man of a Thousand Voices" Mel Blanc performed one evening, telling jokes and then regaling the audience as Bugs Bunny and all the other beloved *Looney Tunes* characters he voiced.

There were a few house bands over the decades: Lenny Herman in the late 1960s and early 1970s. Joey Dale and his band for many years in the 70s and early 80s, playing the hits like *"Tie a Yellow Ribbon Round the Old Oak Tree."* In the late 80s and 90s, Prime Time, led

The house band Prime Time taking over the stage at a Wednesday Night Dinner

by Danny Dalelio and Cathy O'Brien, with a consistent repertoire including Miami Sound Machine, Swing Out Sister's *"Breakout"* and *"The Time of My Life"* – an appropriate reference to the very Dirty Dancing-like vibes of the summer evening. Some members, feeling the music, would get up to dance. Carole D, a member there with her family, remembers how fun it was getting called onto the stage by Joey Dale for a serenade one evening. Other evenings might turn into karaoke, members getting on stage to belt their own renditions with the accompanying band.

Occasionally though, especially in the early days, the show was a bit more risqué, and it was clear why the kids were kicked out. There would be burlesque shows, and belly dancers who brought men on stage to join in the fun. One such man was Dean Horowitz. Dean and his wife Edith were longtime members, and their son Alan – a close friend of my father's – was a cabana boy in the 1970s. One night, Dean had a few too many drinks, as he had a tendency to do, and jumped up on stage with the belly dancer where he proceeded to drop his pants in front of 800 fellow members. Edith wasn't the same after that. Their son Alan, who had gone to the diner across the street with a few of the other cabana boys, was spared the image, but he heard the stories immediately afterward and still holds the memory of his father's claim to fame. Wednesday evenings at the Palms were always evenings to remember.

The appetite for delicious Palms Shore Club meals was clearly insatiable – even when members did *have* to pay. And so other options evolved over the years. In the 1980s, Grandpa Bob decided to offer Sunday Night Dinners: members would place their orders during the day, and in the evening, the hot meals would be delivered to them by their cabana boys. The offering evolved a bit in the 1990s to mirror the popular and flexible Wednesday evenings: these Sunday Night BBQs were served buffet-styles, with large grills and tempting tables of food, this time set up on the back sports courts.

My grandparents put a fun spin on the BBQs, by requiring that the offerings be paid for with "funny money," aka poker chips that could be bought with cash at the start of the buffet line, where members would tally up how much they needed to purchase their favorites on the menu board. Say $20 in chips for spare ribs, BBQ chicken and sides. They'd use the chips to 'buy' the food they wanted at the buffet tables; far too often sending their kids or husbands back to get more "funny money", when they realized they'd underestimated their appetites. Lucky ones, like my sister and cousins Jenine and Nicole, would subtly bypass the long line, poking their heads around the fence from the adjacent courts, for Uncle Mel to pass them a plate with a burger and fries. While there wasn't as much food-piling or tinfoil leftovers as the free Wednesday dinners, the BBQ food and ambience still made for a popular end-of-weekend ritual.

Members loved to delegate cooking dinner to the Palms, and the Jewish members in particular were excited by the Friday Night Takeouts that were offered in the 1980s and 90s. Instead of having to think about Shabbat dinner, they could put in an order when they got to the Palms on Friday morning –a whole chicken, brisket, challah, and more – and the delicious meal would be ready to pick up at the snack bar when they left in the late afternoon, ready to be heated and thrown on the table.

The 'Nightclub': From Day to Night

Have you ever had a 'real' cherry coke? Coca-cola mixed with grenadine – pure, sugary deliciousness. It was one of my favorite parts of going to parties at the Palms Shore Club. I'd run up to the bar on the edge of the enormous Palm Room, the top floor of the hall, and with my head just peeking above the counter, shyly ask Letitia to make me a drink – most often a cherry coke, maybe a Shirley Temple. It was a very different bar – and a very different vibe – than when the Palms first opened its doors.

When the Palms Shore Club first opened in the 1960s, the hall had a very different purpose: it was a bustling, year-round nightclub offering dining and live entertainment. That's what made the Palms unique. There were a few other cabana clubs starting to make their mark in the New York region at the time, but the Palms wasn't *just* another summer retreat—it was *"an unusual dining and swimming spa"* and *"the first cabana club-night club arrangement in the borough,"* according to local Brooklyn newspapers. The two floors of entertaining space had beautiful views overlooking the pools and cabana club, out to

A 1962 write-up on the Palms dining and entertainment – found in the box of Palms Shore Club mementos, likely from the New York Journal-American, a daily newspaper published until 1966

The 'Nightclub': From Day to Night

brooklyn after dark
with Joe Neglia

The luxurious splendor of the world's playgrounds close by the rippling blue Mediterranean is more than adequately rivalled by Bob Burfood's breathtaking Palms Shore Club overlooking the tranquil waters of Our Town's world renowned Sheepshead Bay.

Fascinating pastel hues accent the exquisite details of the modern architecture which surrounds the beautifully designed Olympic-sized pool, comfortable cabanas and outdoor furnishings.

A Cook's Tour of the interior brings us to the Rattan Room — as spellbinding as any nitery on Broadway. The sheer artistry of the decor, top quality entertainment, expertly prepared cuisine, the lavishly decorated and well-stocked bar, the relaxing atmosphere of soft music and the unparalleled service, all tend to make Bob Burfond's dream of a Riviera-like nitery in Brooklyn come true.

The entire setup is as though some good fairy just snapped her wand and with one magic word, deposited this almost unbelievably beautiful structure of entertainment and relaxation right smack in our midst.

With a capacity of 400, the facilities of the Rattan Room are available for catering purposes. Whatever the occasion, the guests are in for a treat well beyond anyone's wildest expectations.

Starting this weekend, Fran Warren and Jackie Kahane will be the star attractions of a Hollywood-type floor show. Larry Best, Alan Dale, Johnny Desmond, Tommy Leonetti, Toni Arden are just a few of Broadway' top show biz stars who are scheduled for appearances at the Palms Shore Club.

Although it won't be a year until this July since the birth of the Palm Shore Club, Bob Burfond can certainly be proud of his achievements — and we, in turn, salute the young congenial host for a job exceedingly well done.

***

STRICTLY AFTER DARK—
Yielding to public demand, Club Inferno, 5th Ave., will feature exotic dancers to headline its shows. The irrepressible Jaja will be in the leadoff spot tonight and Saturday — and our guess is that it won't be long ere Club Inferno will be popularly referred to as the House of the Belly Dancers... The famous Isley Brothers will be featured this weekend at the Town Hill, Eastern Pkwy... Ever get aces back-to-back? Well, Ralph Chiara, Club 18's enterprising young host, will present Ricky Vallo this weekend and follow this sensational Brooklyn recording star with Kakota Staton next week. Top Notch entertainment in anybody's book... Rose Liran, dynamic song stylist from the land of Israel will make her Brooklyn debut tonight at Pip's Lounge, Sheepshead Bay.

** *

BROOKLYN IS BIG LEAGUE — The tingling sounds of a drum especially when Jerry Vincent is manipulating the sticks in his own unforgettable manner... Jackie Brooks King of the Ivories at the West End Lounge... Joe Coniglio and his entire

---

Fit For Kings
A GUIDE TO GOURMET DINING IN BROOKLYN

Persons who have been going out more but enjoying it less need be informed of the Palma Shore Club in Sheepshead Bay, an elaborate, exquisite night-life spot guaranteed to make for a memorable evening.

If driving and parking complications and mediocre food and service have repelled Brooklynites from attempting an evening "uptown," they will welcome the knowledge that there is — in their own borough — a place offering a full evening, complete with dinner, drinks, a show, dancing, and plenty of "atmosphere."

Like the man said, "Who can ask for anything more?"

Located at Emmons Ave. and Ford St., overlooking Sheepshead Bay, the Palms Shore Club is unique in providing "what Brooklyn really needs in the form of entertainment," according to affable manager Abe Kasten.

An evening at the club will prove that Mr. Kasten is certainly not prone to overstatement.

Excluding Mondays, continuous dancing and two shows nightly are featured, with three performances on Saturdays. Sal Scari is the capable musical director of Palms Shore's two bands.

The club seeks to "import" name stars, and this week highlighted comedian Georgie Kay and Paramount recording star Maxine Brown, held over for an extended stay in the Rattan Room are the fabulous McClevertys, a lively, colorful group of calypso dancers and singers.

Testifying to the popularity of the nightclub and the prominence of its performers, it was noted by Mr. Kasten that when singer Jerry Vale appeared two weeks ago, the Palm Room was forced to close its doors to three audiences; the club was that filled.

From Nov. 29–Dec. 5, Lou Nelson, Patti Prince, and Eileen and Jack Stewart will be performing. The show goes on at 9 and 11:30; on Saturdays, showtime is 9, 11:30, and 1:30. Dinner is served from 6.

Able maitre d' Jack Harris takes the reservations at SH 3-4444. For information concerning banquet arrangements and party functions, persons are advised to contact Mildred Miller at the same number.

A member of American expresso and the Diner's Club, Palms Shore was opened last July on an idea by owner Bob Herfond to herald in a new concept in Brooklyn nite life. As a result, not only does Palms Shore include a night club and cocktail lounge, facilities for seating a total of 600, a capacious parking lot and free valet parking, but also a plush cabana club (more of which to come in a future issue.)

Palms Shore thus emerges as the first cabana club-night club arrangement in the borough. As part of the recent expansion program, the club witnessed the advent of a dancing studio and a beauty salon. By 1963, Mr. Kasten pointed out, a snack bar and coffee shop will be installed.

A gala New Year's Eve affair is planned; $20 per person will cover a scrumptious sirloin dinner and all favors. An all-star show is being planned.

All in all, taking onto consideration the expanded facilities, the spacious parking area, the impressive surroundings, the star-studded show, the dancing, the fine music, the prompt service, and the A-1 food, if the Palms Shore Club can't satisfy you, no night spot can.

Write-ups in regular newspaper columns extolling the dining and entertainment at the Palms in the early 1960s: "Fit For Kings" - Kings Courier, December 1962; "Brooklyn After Dark" – Brooklyn Eagle, March 1963

A faded postcard inviting guests to the new Palms Shore Club nightclub in the 1960s

Sheepshead Bay, through the wall of tall windows, connecting the two worlds. At that time, there were even stairs that led straight from the lower pool deck into the hall, making the day-to-night transition effortless for cabana members during the summer.

The top floor, named the Palm Room right from the start, was truly *the* place for entertainment, a hotspot where 200 to 300 guests would crowd in to see a range of popular and talented comedians, singers, and musicians. Under the leadership of Maître D' Neil Kasman from the mid-1960s and later Julie Erlich in the 1970s – with the support of talent agent Charles Rapp – they succeeded in bringing in some of the biggest names of the day to perform for the Brooklyn audience. Especially Jewish entertainers, making the Palms an epicenter for this talent outside of the Borscht Belt.

Performers included singers like Alan Dale, Jerry Butler, Johnny Desmond, Don Cornell, and chart-topper Jerry Vale; comedians like Buddy Hackett, Bernie Allen, Jackie Mason and Morty Gunty. When

The 'Nightclub': From Day to Night

The packed entertainment program for a summer, as captured in the Palms Shore Tattler

not on *The Tonight Show* or *The Ed Sullivan Show*, the hilarious Totie Fields was a regular and well-loved Palms performer. All-around entertainer Sal Richards performed with his brother, singer Steve Diamond. Jimmy Dean, the celebrated singer and TV host– perhaps best-known today for his eponymous sausage brand – performed his number one Billboard hit "Big Bad John". Soap opera star Eileen

Fulton premiered her newest single, "As The World Turns," at the Palms, and The Soul Survivors performed their soon-to-be hit "Expressway to Your Heart". Comedian Jackie Mason, in between Broadway appearances, took the stage at the Palms, even finding time to hit on some of the guests. (One young woman recalled that after his performance, Mason declared she was "the woman of his dreams," to which she quipped back, "I'm sure you have many dreams.")

Bob Berfond, the Palms Shore Club congenial host with Sal Sicari the clubs musical director and Neil Kasman, Maitre D of the Palms were recent guests of Joe Franklin, host of T.V. "Memory Lane".

Grandpa Bob and the nightclub team promoting the Palms on Joe Franklin's Memory Lane, as captured in the Palms Shore Tattler

And on and on it went. The entertainers would take the stage—singers backed by Sal Sicari and his orchestra—centered in the spotlight by Billy M or a young man such as cousin Larry Berfond, working the large followspot from the back room.

Picture *The Marvelous Mrs. Maisel*: women in tea-length dresses and men in suits, eager for an

Advertisement for Palms Shore Club events – only $5 per person! – in The Tablet in Nov 1963

evening of fine dining and live entertainment, happy to pay the $5 or so for a night out while leaving the kids at home. They would drop off their hats, coats and cares with Ginger in the checkroom, and make their way into the high-ceilinged Palm Room with the curved floor-to ceiling windows to meet friends. They'd sit at the long tables, laughing and chatting, men lighting their cigars, before the entertainment began. Waiters took drink orders throughout the evening, keeping tabs at the bustling service bar in the back, manned by my teenaged dad and Uncle Mel in the 1970s, with cocktail waitresses ferrying drinks to the table.

Palm Room set up for rare large private events in the 1960s and 1970s

As Joe Neglia described in 1963 in his regular *Brooklyn Daily Eagle* column 'Brooklyn After Dark', *"Despite all of the rave notices for its week-after-week of top notch show biz talent, the Palms Shore Club doubles in spades as one of the finest and most alluring dining palaces in Our Town."*

Guests often reserved one or two tables at these public events for group celebrations. Friday evenings were often designated for Sweet Sixteens, where each birthday girl would sit among friends and family at a long table, enjoying a three-course meal and the evening's entertainment. They would join five or six other girls to blow out candles at a line of cake tables set up on the dance floor, while the whole room joined in a chorus of *Happy Birthday*. Then the busboys would present each of them with flowers. With so many pretty young ladies, the teenage waiters and busboys were almost as excited as the guests.

A keepsake photograph holder from the popular New Years Eve in September, Labor Day 1964 (courtesy of Nancy Gordon)

Brian Lawrence, a waiter in the 1970s, remembered nervously serving soup to the girls and their parents, trying to balance the hefty 30-pound tureen while ladling steaming bowls, terrified of spilling on a guest and ruining any chance of getting a girl's phone number later—a definite perk of the job. Eric Yorke, a busboy around the same time, actually met his future wife of over 40 years, Mona, when she had her *Sweet Sixteen* at the Palms in 1974 – even though at the time, he was dating one of her friends.

Saturday nights would be a more broadly festive atmosphere, with different tables celebrating different occasions – a birthday or bat mitzvah here, an engagement or anniversary there.

Another festive end-of-season New Years Eve in September in 1967, as captured in the Palms Shore Tattler

In the mid-1960s, the Palms became an early adopter of the popular 'discotheque' concept, playing recorded music instead of live musicians for an evening of fun and dancing. Silent films from decades earlier were projected onto the walls to add to the ambiance of light and motion. Grandpa Bob's younger cousin, Andy Berfond, remembered being sent out to Long Island with his newly acquired driver's license to pick up the film reels from the one small business that rented them out.

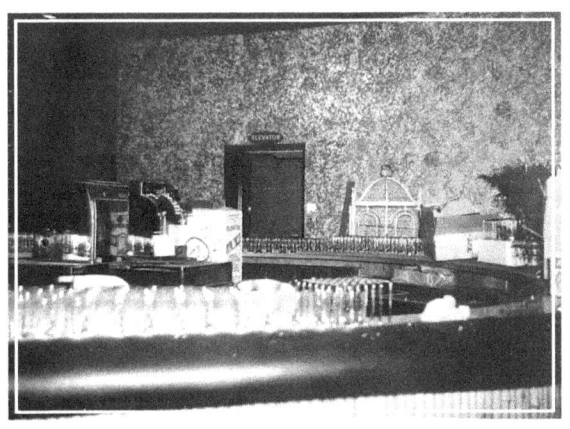

The impressive round bar in the Rattan Room, when the Palms was first built in June 1962

The Palm Room was also host to some extravagant annual celebrations beloved by the cabana club members. New Year's Eve was always a blowout, packed with guests enjoying the top quality food, flowing liquor, music and dancing late into the night. The same festive energy came each summer with the members-only 'New Year's Eve in September' and Fourth of July extravaganza. There were other evening activities dedicated for cabana club members as well: Smorgasbord and Champagne Hours, dance contests, themed evenings like Latin Fiestas and Hawaiian Luaus.

The view from the Rattan Room bar out to the cabana club, with a cameo from Jekyll or Heckle in the birdcage, in the 1960s

The Palms Shore Club

Members enjoy dancing "The Alley Cat", Friday Nights in the Palm Room!

Members dancing the evening away in the Palm Room in 1965, as captured in the Palms Shore Tattler

The middle floor, known as the Rattan Room, was smaller and more of a cocktail lounge, centered around a grand circular bar. Open to the public, it became a common meeting place for, let's say, some *connected* gentlemen. This was the domain of Frankie Cass, the bartender, who – like a character straight out of a mob movie – held court while confidently pouring drinks for his buddies. Cousin Andy, working in the adjacent snack bar during the Palms' first few years, remembered weaving through the bar patrons to reach the storage room on the other side, to grab more plates, cups, napkins, doing his best not to make eye contact or overhear too much of the conversation. But avoiding those conversations wasn't always possible. In the late 1960s, Grandpa Bob decided the lounge needed birds because, well, why not? He bought a large ornate cage and welcomed to the family Heckle and Jekyll, a pair of talking mynas. The result was predictable: the birds

Dance evenings for members in the 1960s (courtesy of Nancy Gordon)

soaked up the language of the bar's clientele and soon filled the room with a constant stream of loud, colorful curses. The ladies were horrified. Needless to say, Heckle and Jekyll did not call the Palms home for long.

Fortunately, the Rattan Room was also host to more refined company. The 100-person space could be booked for private functions. Weddings, and the occasionally large Bar Mitzvah. The $12-$15 per person price tag was steep for the time but included nearly everything: colored linens, French service, rolling bar, gratuities, valet parking, flowers, candles, coat check, and more. Waiters shuttled food down from the main kitchen upstairs —a task made easier once a dumbwaiter was installed. A house band provided the music, pausing only for courses to be served.

The Rattan Room was also a go-to spot for neighborhood groups hosting luncheons, meetings, awards dinners, benefit galas, and fundraising dances. From women's society chapters and charity groups to political clubs and precinct community councils, all turned to the Palms to host their events, often advertising in the local papers. There were even singles mixers hosted by the aptly named organization, "Come Together."

Cousin Philip and Uncle Mel working as busboys, in the classic red jackets, in the late 1970s

No matter the event, top-notch service remained the Palms' trademark. It did create an intense environment for the staff: eager teenage busboys in red jackets and bow ties, and older, unionized waiters in gold jackets—led for decades by the hardworking but curmudgeonly head waiter Marty and his kind right-hand man, Frank Bucari. Some busboys eventually earned their gold jackets, but all learned invaluable lessons, not only how to efficiently cut a round cake, but also life skills around working hard and acting professionally.

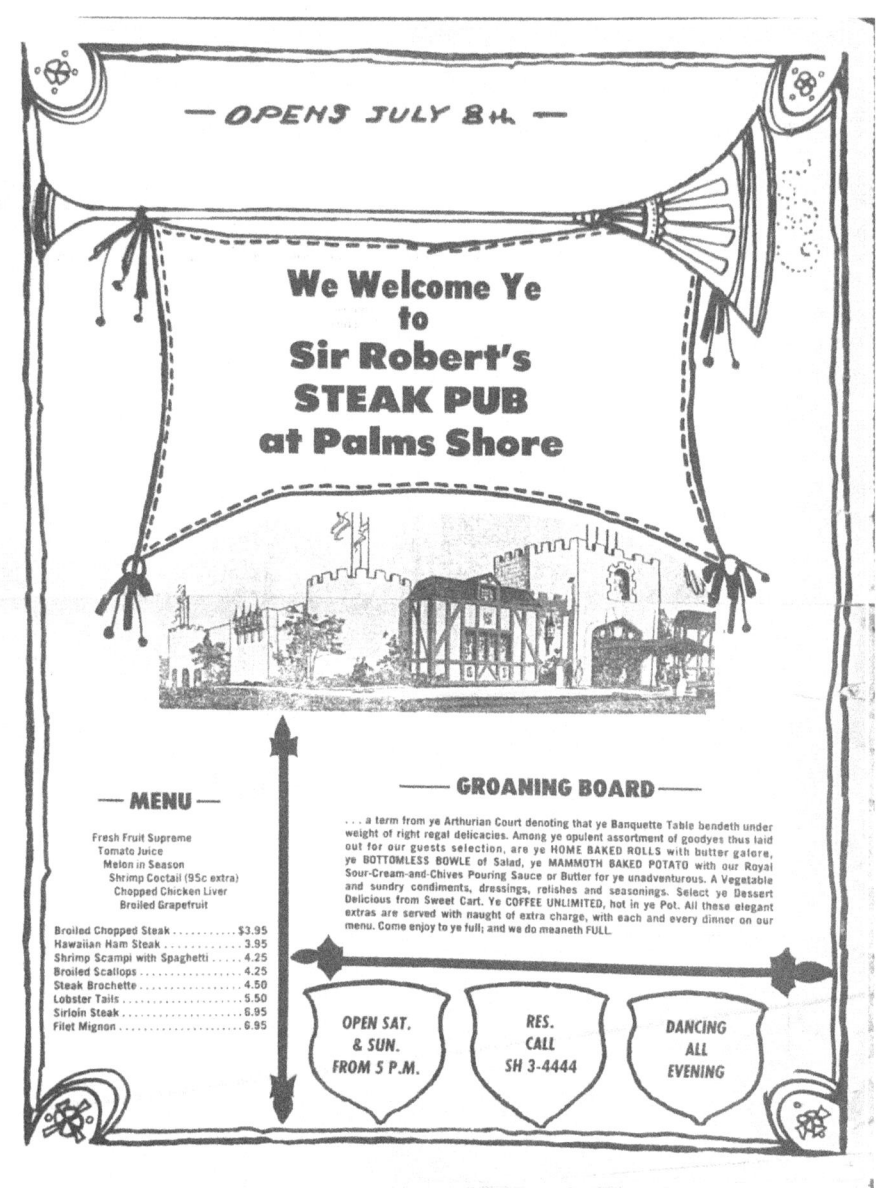

Advertisement for Sir Roberts Steak Pub in the 1960s, as captured in the Palms Shore Tattler

Eric Yorke recalled arguing with the strict head chef, Mr. Ong, and storming out of the kitchen cursing him. When Mr. Ong came charging after him, cleaver in hand, my dad intervened to defuse the situation and offer a lesson: it didn't matter if Eric was technically right. "There are lots of waiters," my dad said, "but only one chef." The takeaway stuck – in life, you have to know who you can yell at, and who you can't.

The job also inspired creativity. Staff consistently looked for ways to make the grueling work easier and more efficient. That ingenuity was modeled by Grandpa Bob himself, who was always experimenting with new ideas. One of his 1960s innovations: Sir Roberts Steak Pub. During the summer, sun-sleepy cabana members could trade their bathing suits for evening clothes and head inside, where the bar floor transformed into a fine dining experience complete with steaks and dancing. The Steak Pub would pop up during several summers through the 1970s and 1980s, with my dad and others pitching in.

No matter the set-up of the room or style of service, the quality of food and the welcoming atmosphere in the multi-level Palms hall remained constant through the 1960s and 1970s, drawing thousands of guests from across Brooklyn.

A Place in the Action: Politics and the Palms

Growing up, I believed my dad could have been a politician. Everyone knew who he was, they wanted to say hello, to be his friend. Whether we were walking the Palms Shore Club premises or dining at a restaurant anywhere in the New York-New Jersey area, people would walk over eagerly, shake his hand or pat his back, and share a compliment or a "thank you," or a funny anecdote about the Palms. My dad would smile and nod, say a few nice words, and introduce me, standing shyly with my hand in his, or half-hidden behind his legs. When they walked away, I would ask him who it was – sometimes getting a fun back-story or quick rundown of their family tree. Other times, he didn't really know them. But no matter the level of connection, I would notice the satisfied smile of those we just met, having bumped into THE Allen Berfond, very much like the reaction any of the actual politicians who frequented the Palms would get.

As membership grew at The Palms Shore Club in the 1960s, it became a prime campaign spot for local politicians. Large numbers of their constituents were already gathered, relaxed, happy, and satiated with food, sun and fun. When John Lindsay ran his winning bid for mayor of New York City in 1965, he spent a July day at the Palms, speaking to the admiring crowd, shaking hands, and signing autographs.

Lindsay was accompanied by none other than the now iconic Liza Minnelli—daughter of Judy Garland (best known for her role as Dorothy Gale in the 1939 The *Wizard of Oz* film) and Vincente Minnelli. At the time, Minnelli was a nineteen-year-old rising star in the New York theater and nightclub scene, and a last-minute replacement for the originally slated entertainer, Sammy Davis Jr. (who was already a major movie and music star and part of Frank Sinatra's Rat

Pack.) Despite having big shoes to fill, Liza did not disappointed in the least – she wowed the crowd with several songs, including "Singing in the Rain," her star-power already unmistakable.She was accompanied by the Lionel Hampton Orchestra, the legendary big band led by one jazz's most influential figures. It was a memorable day at the Palms.

Even without celebrity performers, many politicians followed in Lindsay's footsteps: future New York City mayors Abraham Beame and Ed Koch during their campaigns in the 1970s and 1980s; U.S. congressmen from New York such as Democratic House Representative Richard L. Ottinger; gubernatorial candidates like Republican Andrew O'Rourke; and a number of long-time local figures, like New York State Attorney General Louis J Lefkowitz. They would park their limos or fancy cars out front and spend hours glad-handing the Palms' cabana club members.

Beyond campaign appearances, some politicians also spent their leisure time at the Palms. Mayor Abraham Beame's family had their own cabana, and the famously short city leader would often come by. Another frequent visitor was long-time New York State Senator Marty Markowitz, who would later go on to become Brooklyn Borough President. Most notably, Meade Esposito, the Brooklyn Democratic leader and political "boss" who wielded immense influence in the 1970s and 1980s, was a frequent guest. While my family didn't formally engage in politics, Grandpa Bob knew the importance of relationships, and with Esposito's connections, the Palms began hosting a growing number of political events.

The Thomas Jefferson Democratic Club and Harry S Truman Democratic Club hosted their annual dinner-dances at the Palms Shore Club throughout the 1970s and 1980s, honoring a range of public figures– from City Councilmen Leon Katz and Herbert Berman to State Assembly members such as Anthony Genovesi, Shirley Weiner and Stanley Fink. Even Mario Cuomo was an honoree at a Palms event in 1982—then just Lieutenant Governor and a potential candidate for governor. The overflow crowd of more than 350 people was perhaps an indicator of his future success, as Cuomo would go on

The Palms Shore Club

LINDSAY AT THE PALMS

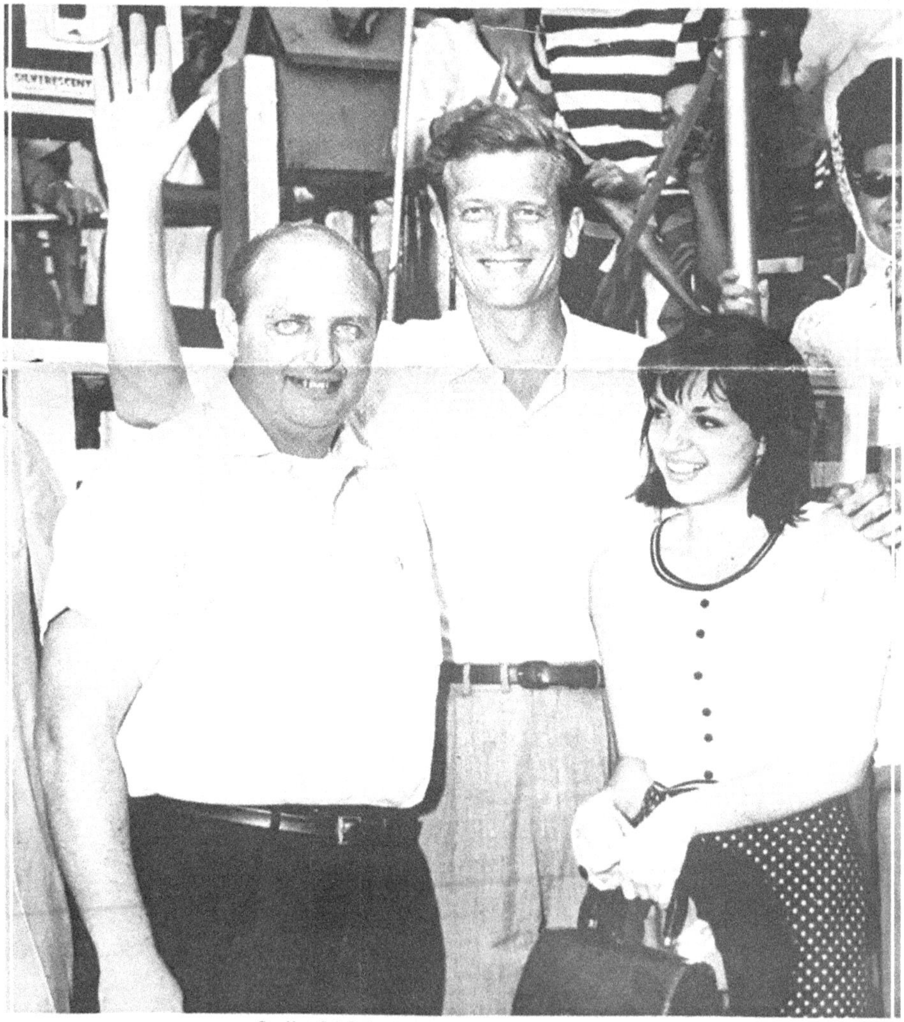

Our Host Bob Berfond greets John Lindsay and Liza Minnelli.
More pictures and story on Page 4

A Place in the Action: Politics and the Palms

The Palms Shore Tattler captures John Lindsay's mayoral campaign visit, with an accompanying performance by rising star Liza Minelli in 1965 (photos by Palms member Howard Gordon)

to serve three terms as governor. The guests always enjoyed the Palms' delicious fare, first-rate entertainment, and warm décor. But more importantly, the Palms became a stage for political theater, a place where crowd size, guest lists, and handshakes often signaled the power dynamics of New York politics.

Ed Koch campaigning at the Palms Shore Club for New York City Mayor in 1982, with Palms lifeguard Paul Rosenblit

There were related events as well—fundraisers, for instance, like a 1981 $50-a-head cocktail party for Councilman Leon Katz that netted around $25,000. The Palms also hosted prominent honorary receptions. More than 400 people gathered in February 1975 to celebrate the retirement of Congressman Frank J. Brasco after four terms representing New York in the U.S. House of Representatives. And in 1985, the Palms held a "Farewell to the Chief" celebration for Meade Esposito himself, drawing prominent borough, city and state officials to honor "one of the most powerful men in New York State politics for over a decade."

Across such events, the Palms regularly welcomed a "who's who" of New York's political scene, many names still recognizable today: Brooklyn Borough President Howard Golden, State Senator Franz Leichter, then-Congressman Charles Schumer, and even Al Gore, when he sought the Democratic Party's presidential nomination in 1988.

With Esposito's recommendations, the Palms also began taking on select off-premises catering for important political events. When New York Supreme Court justices and other notable judges were sworn in at Borough Hall, Palms food and staff were there for the celebratory dinners and cocktail parties.

A Place in the Action: Politics and the Palms

The culmination came with the Brooklyn Democratic Party's massive fundraiser in May 1979, honoring Howard Golden—the largest event the Palms ever undertook. The Party rented Pier 85

Canarsie Courier article on a gala honoring Democratic Party boss Meade Esposito, held at the Palms in March 1985

overlooking the Hudson River on Manhattan's West Side, sold tickets to more than 2,000 guests, and hired the Palms Shore Club to manage the extravagant evening. Of course, Grandpa Bob said yes, and it became an all-hands-on-deck operation. Under the theme "Foods of the World", the meal was staged as an international buffet—two tables each for Chinese, Indian, Italian, Greek, and other cuisines, complete with heaping platters and themed decorations. The Palms provided as much food as it could prepare, while outsourcing other specialties to local Brooklyn restaurants, including Mei Mei's, a famous Chinese eatery on Nostrand Avenue.

My dad went to pick up the food from Mei Mei's, piling pots and trays of chow mein, rice and egg rolls into the truck – the hardest part, he said, was schlepping the heavy dishes onto the pier. There were also six enormous bars set-up across the pier, each stocked with crates and crates of liquor. Fortunately, the Palms staff had a full 24hours of access beforehand, and they needed every moment.

Part of the setup was arranging more than two hundred floral centerpieces. That task fell to the Palms' fastidious florist, Mike Andriano – known to everyone as "Wrecker," though I never learned why. Wrecker brought in several other florists to help, and the crew worked through the night to meet his high standards. Grandpa Bob assigned his middle son, my uncle Mel, who was about nineteen-years-old at the time, as point-person, to supervise the florists and the rest of the overnight prep team. It was nearing 5a.m. when the florists finally finished up and asked Uncle Mel for payment. But Grandpa Bob hadn't left his son with any money or instructions. The florists, exhausted and aware of Grandpa Bob's reputation for slow payments (especially to vendors), were furious. According to Uncle Mel, one of the men grabbed him by the shirt, pressed a floral cutting knife to his neck, and demanded he get the money.

Shaken, Uncle Mel found a pay phone —this was long before cell phones— and called his father at home, waking him. With his son threatened, Grandpa Bob reluctantly agreed to get out of bed, and meet the florists at the Palms Shore Club to hand over the well-earned cash. Uncle Mel was safe, and the floral centerpieces turned out beautifully, but it was a night that none of them would forget.

Fortunately, the event itself went off without a hitch, an incredible feat. It was, however, an exhausting day for everyone involved. Around 200 people were hired to work that day – regular Palms staff, family and friends – to serve food to the mingling politicians, donors, and well-to-do Brooklynites who breezed through for an hour or two of schmoozing. For all the preparation and effort, the event was over in a flash. While it was certainly memorable, it would also be the last large-scale off-site event the Palms ever catered. In subsequent years, the Brooklyn Democratic Party opted for simpler hotel venues, much to the relief of Grandpa Bob and everyone else.

A Teenage Home Base

I can still feel the low but consistent hum of jealousy that coursed through my preteen body in my last few summers at the Palms Shore Club. While I loved spending time with my grandparents and cousins, and even my alone time, it was hard not to be distracted by the cliques of beautiful teenagers that roamed around the Palms like they owned the place. Some were members; others were staff on break from work. I'd sneakily watch the cute shirtless guys and effortlessly cool girls in colorful bikinis, flirting and joking, moving in groups around the premises. The Palms closed before I was old enough to even attempt to be part of such a group, but I could see the central role this place played in a perfect teenage summer.

The Palms cabana club was an ideal summer home for Sheepshead Bay's teenagers. There were dozens of teenage cabana boys, lifeguards, camp counselors and snack bar staff who all worked hard but had plenty of time off the clock. And then there were the teenage members, too old for the day camp but not yet ready to take their place at the mahjong tables. The result was interweaving groups of youth roving in and around the Palms Shore Club, under the spell of summer heat and hormones, eager to have fun.

During the day, the teenage members would often gather in groups for a casual summer routine. While their parents were playing cards and younger siblings were in camp, they might lounge around or play sports or grab snacks and sit by the marina. Some of the girls took on 'mother's helper' or babysitting jobs, watching over the babies and toddlers for a few hours a day so their moms could focus on important tasks of tanning and table games. It wasn't a bad gig – the teens could earn a decent amount of money while hanging out with each other, pushing around strollers or letting the kids play together. Rachael Newman Komissaroff remembers how she and her friends found an empty area of the former Luau Room, and let the babies crawl around in the enclosed space – their own informal baby camp. In the afternoons, they might leave for a walk or bite out in the neighborhood, before coming back to relax, using the Palms Shore Club essentially as a home base until they were kicked out at the end of day.

The young members would be joined by the teenage staff when they were on break or after hours, and were quick to find ways to have fun. Grabbing food or drinks from the snack bar, playing paddleball and stickball, competing against the older members in volleyball and water polo games, or playing pranks on each other and others (like holding an informal and inappropriate "weigh-in" contest for one of the larger men at the club). The opportunity to be outside, to take advantage of the amenities during breaks, was a considerable perk of a job at the Palms.

And as one would expect, when you get a bunch of young men and women together, there were also less-innocent activities. As with the members, card games were a popular pastime, and many cabana boys credit the Palms with teaching or honing their gambling skills. The cabana boys who "ran" the poker games would observe the techniques of the older players during the day, and practice their newfound skills in the evenings against their peers.

Captain Walters, the popular bar on Emmons Avenue that young people from the Palms would frequent after closing

The mat room – where the lounge chairs and mats were stored – was the go-to spot for first joints, sneaked-in-bottles of liquor, and other illicit substances. Despite the lingering smell of pot and mildew, it was also a popular spot for first kisses and more-than-innocent fooling around. Though the mat room was certainly not the only option for coupling and carousing. They'd scope out any unlocked or unused cabanas. They'd take over the paddleball courts when the older members tired of playing, as the tall walls provided a solid hideaway.

There were also some sanctioned activities specifically for the teenagers. While Wednesday Night Dinners were for the adults, the Palms also hosted members-only "Teen Nights" on Thursdays. On these popular evenings, the parents would pack up and take the younger kids home, while their teenagers stayed back for a carefree summer evening. As the Palms was a trusted environment, parents were happy to leave teenagers as young as 13, returning hours later

Cousin Larry and his band Smile performing at a Teen Night in 1968, wearing their Beatles-inspired flowered shirts; from left-to-right, Larry Berfond on bass, Phyllis Ricardi on drums, Jan Owen on guitar, and Doug Bittner on keyboard

for car-pooled pickups. And the teens were more than happy to spend the evening with friends, enjoying a free dinner and dancing to the latest music of the day, without any judging adult stares. In 1963, Grandpa Bob even brought in Bruce Morrow – a well-known radio personality on WABC at that time – as MC and director for a summer schedule of teenage shows. In the late '60s, Cousin "Big Larry" and his band *Smile* performed at Teen Nights, earning very little but getting some solid exposure.

Then there was after-hours. The young staff in particular felt they had 24/7 access to the cabana club, rightly or wrongly. Some would go early in the morning, and eat breakfast while overlooking Sheepshead Bay. Others would stay late at night, like Barry Weinstein in the early 1970s, raiding the snack bar to make sandwiches and then going fishing out in the Bay. Brian Lawrence, a cabana boy a few years later, remembers sleeping there a number of nights, taking liberties by crashing in some of the higher-end patio cabanas, resting, showering, and getting ready for the next day of work.

Most often, after closing, the teenage staff and members would leave in large groups to go out together. Some of them would pile into cars and head to Roosevelt Raceway or another nearby racetrack. But usually, they would stay in the neighborhood. Whether celebrating a water polo win, or just looking for an evening out to party, they would invade and essentially take over a local restaurant or bar. Like Jahn's, a diner within walking-distance popular for dessert, including the famous 'kitchen sink' – an appropriately named silver tub filled with ice cream scoops and toppings. There was always Wheelers, an unassuming bar around the corner on Sheepshead Bay Road (still there to this day), or Captain Walter's, another neighborhood watering hole at Emmons Ave. and Bedford Ave. And the ever-popular Midwood Lounge, a pizzeria a short drive away on Kings Highway, with a jukebox and a hopping bar under the watch of one-eyed owner Louie. The group would stay out until the early morning hours, often wreaking havoc. In their teenage minds, they were royalty, and the Palms Shore Club was their summer domain.

My Uncle Mel, in his late teens at the time, got in his first and only bar fight at Midwood Lounge one of these evenings. It's unclear who started it, but suddenly Uncle Mel and his friends, Mitch Alkon and Ronald Kestenbaum, all coming off a full day of work, were fully at war with a few strangers at the bar – pushing, punching, climbing on each other's backs, throwing chairs. The owner stepped in, and kicked the other men out of the bar; given how much they spent, the Berfonds weren't the ones to be tossed out. It only cemented, for the other teens, the stature of belonging to this informal but powerful Palms Shore Club fraternity.

THE 'HEY DAY' OF THE 1970S, EMBEDDING THE PALMS IN BROOKLYN HISTORY

A Tribute to the Community: Salute to Israel and Festa Italiana

The perfect texture of a matzo ball, in my opinion, is spongy but with a slight firmness at its core. And then it needs to be sitting in a salty (but not too salty), flavorful chicken broth. The Palms always knew how to make this ideal matzo ball soup, perhaps one of the main reasons I always loved our family's Passover seders. In the final years of the Palms, I remember slurping down the soup in the Rattan Room, where we had informal private family celebrations, all of the Berfond grandchildren racing around to find the afikomen in the vast space. But when I was very young, we took a table or two at larger community seders in the Palm Room upstairs, where a rabbi would lead a more formal seder over the delicious meal for a few dozen Jewish families. I got to be part of something bigger – a tradition that through the 1980s and early 90s was a way to engage the Palms Shore Club's large Jewish community. And as I've learned, not the only such tribute to its Jewish roots.

Grandpa Bob was always looking to attract customers outside of the summer season, and in 1970, he hit on a new idea: multi-week themed celebrations. 'Salute to Israel' and 'Festa Italiana', tributes to the largely Jewish and Italian Brooklyn families frequenting the

Palms, became annual mainstays in the 1970s and early 1980s. For three weeks each, between January and March, both floors of the Palms event space were transformed into these two immersive cultural experiences. Upon entering the main floor, there was artwork and exhibits for the guests to peruse, and vendor displays of crafts, fashion and accessories. While browsing, they would sip on glasses of wine, and nibble on passed hors d'oeuvres. They'd put in their entries for door prizes and free raffles, and then head upstairs for the main event.

A Tribute to the Community: Salute to Israel and Festa Italiana

Pages from a printed package marking the first season of Salute to Israel in 1970

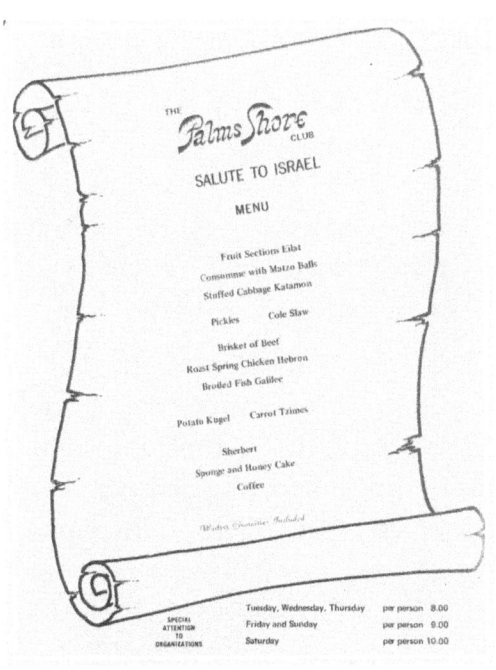

In the Palms Room, there would be music and dancing, "star-studded" entertainment, fashion shows, and themed dinners. Weeknights and weekends alike, the events drew diverse crowds – couples and families from the broader Palms network, community groups seeking destinations for celebrations or fundraisers. And as with all of Grandpa Bob's endeavors, he went all in: the food, the décor, the entertainment, were tailored to the theme. Even the staff attire, whether sashes and hats or full costumes courtesy of Grandma Gloria, was part of the cultural immersion, though by today's standards, not always culturally sensitive.

The Palms Shore Club

Advertisements for Fiesta Italiana and Salute to Israel in the Daily News, April 1970 and February 1974

"Salute to Israel" usually came first in the year. The event would feature notable performers – from Neva Small, star of *Fiddler on the Roof,* to Israeli singer and comedian Moti Giladi, to the "internationally famous" Ayalons. The menu was kosher-style, highlighting Jewish favorites like matzo ball soup and potato kugel, and brisket. Much of the programming celebrated the vibrancy and growth of modern Israel, though sometimes in unusual ways. One year, Grandpa Bob made my dad stand at the front dressed in very non-politically correct Middle Eastern robes. Another year featured a fashion show where the women modeled bathing suits from the Israeli company Gottex.

"Festa Italiana" was just as elaborate. Guests were greeted at the door with mini glasses of wine and, some years, by young men dressed as Italian soldiers. While browsing, they sampled different varieties of cheese, enjoyed wine tastings, and watched an organ grinder with a monkey perform. Upstairs, they laughed with comics like Joe Carey and Ray Canale, and were serenaded by crooners like Jerry Vale and Jimmy Roselli, along with headliners all the way from Italy — like Mario Da Vinci, Giacomo Rondinella and Emilio Pericoli. The Italian community from across New York City lined up for tickets, including, quietly, a few "wise guys." Guests were treated not only to Palms' food and drink but also to a display of offerings from Italian companies, like Ferraro Foods' specialties and Alitalia's travel promotions.

While the festivals were a highlight for several years, like many of the Palms' innovations, they captured a particular moment in Brooklyn's cultural history. Along with the nightclub, they were phased out before the end of the decade – making way for the next wave of Berfond creativity.

Advertisement for the 1975 Festa Italiana, with edits by Grandma Gloria for the following year

The Unspoken: Mob Members at the Palms

When I was young, I used to wonder if my family was part of the Mafia—the Jewish Mafia, of course. There was something about the way my grandpa quietly but authoritatively oversaw his domain of the Palms Shore Club; the way my uncle Larry wore his gold chains and spoke in that gruff, commanding tone; the way my dad always "knew a guy" who could help; the way things sometimes mysteriously operated at the Palms. The undercurrent around the Berfond men just seemed to match the mob movies my dad loved – they felt like a bunch of Goodfellas. Needless to say, there is no Jewish Mafia (that I know of), and in any case, my family was not part of it. But perhaps I wasn't entirely wrong to sense something, because before I was born, there really was—if only quietly—a Mafia presence at the Palms Shore Club.

11 Are Arrested at 'Las Vegas Night'

Ten men and a woman were arrested early yesterday by the police public morals division in a raid on a "Las Vegas Night" gambling operation at the Palms Shore Beach Club, 3128 Emmons Avenue, Brooklyn. The officers confiscated $6,700 in the raid, which saw 300 people playing cards, dice and a lottery. Those arrested were said to be operating illegally by taking cuts out of the bets made.

Metropolitan Brief describing the raid in the NY Times on August 22, 1976

One night in August 1976, the police raided the Palms Shore Club. It was a Las Vegas Night, a fun evening of gambling hosted by a well-established Brooklyn church with around 300 people playing blackjack, craps, poker, and a lottery. At 1:30 a.m., the festivities were interrupted by an announcement over the public address system: "Be calm. This is a police raid." As captured in newspapers the next day, around twenty undercover officers who had been posing as players suddenly sprang into action, seizing $6,700 in cash and arresting eleven people—including the priest.

The articles reported that the raid followed a three-month investigation by the Brooklyn Organized Crime Bureau's Public Morals Division, which determined that this wasn't just an innocent church-sponsored, casino-themed event. In reality, the operation was tied to illegal gambling run by one of New York's Mafia crime families.

Fortunately, none of my family were among those arrested. My dad, Allen, had left early after being tipped off by organizers who sensed something was wrong—that there were "players" who didn't look familiar.

This wasn't the first casino night at the Palms. Informal gambling had been going on for years, often once or twice a week in the few years leading up to the raid. Buses would pull up out front and men would unload craps and card tables while cabana club members looked on—excited for the lively evening and unconcerned by the event's likely but unspoken Mafia ties. That was how it generally went in Brooklyn at the time. Through the 1970s, the borough was heavily under the influence of the notorious "Five Families" of the Italian-American Mafia. While their power was most visible in certain industries—like the infamous control of garbage collection—their reach extended throughout society. They weren't shy about it either. Members from across the Mafia hierarchy – the bosses, *consiglieres*, made men, and associates – would socialize often and openly, drinking and partying at the city's hottest spots. And in its hey-day, one of those spots was the Palms Shore Club.

From the early days, some of the guests at the Palms were part of the so-called Mafia. Members and associates of some families would convene at the bar, spend evenings in the nightclub, or book private events.

The bosses of two families hosted several of their own parties at the Palms over the years. Sometimes they'd ask the DJ to turn the music up loud, to drown out the whispered conversations in the corners and make sure no nearby FBI agents could pick up their signals. They always tipped him well at the end of the night. Another crime family boss once dropped by the Palms after coming off of a docked boat for lunch. A few wives or mistresses of the extended crime families were cabana club members, so the men would occasionally stop by, even hosting cabana parties when one of their own got out of jail.

With such an acknowledged Mafia presence, it's no surprise that rumor spread. Some believed the Mafia ran or financed the Palms — or at least had a stake in part of the business. Others assumed there must be some kind of "arrangement." But this level of influence, as intriguing as it sounds, wasn't the reality. The Palms was simply one of Brooklyn's most popular venues, a place to see and be seen, whether you were connected or not.

In *Wiseguys*, the non-fiction bestseller that inspired *Goodfellas*, the Palms is even mentioned as a date-night destination for protagonist Henry Hill, a Mafia associate-turned-informant with the Lucchese Family.

The Mafia was just a part of Brooklyn life in the '60s, '70s and even into the '80s. At the Palms, almost everyone knew who the "made men" were, but nobody asked questions—and nobody cared. Beyond the gambling nights, and of course the infamous raid, their presence was subtle: an undercurrent, a shadow of power that became fodder for gossip that traveled between staff and members.

Like the rumor about a former Palms waiter who was allegedly found in the trunk of a car in Staten Island—cut up—for sleeping with a wise guy's wife. Numerous other stories remain off-book, living only in the whispered, possibly embellished memories of those who were there. Still, these tales add to the mythic aura of the Palms—and to its rightful place in Brooklyn history.

The Luau Room: From the World Fair to Disco Hideaway and Beyond

I knew it as the 'mini mall'— an enclosed space in the middle of the Palms Shore Club, beneath my grandparents' elevated house – that served as a throughway to the back patios and Sheepshead Bay marina. In my memory, there was a boutique and a salon – two spaces which I barely set foot in – and a game room, with about twenty arcade games, where I spent hours perfecting my Ms. Pac-Man Skills and trying to beat the scores of the older kids. Fortunately, Grandma Gloria equipped me with rolls of 'slugs' – fake quarters that could trick the machines and feed my gaming habit at no cost. (My attachment ran so deep that when the Palms Shore Club closed, that machine was one of the few things that made its way to our family home in New Jersey.) Despite all the time I spent there, I had no idea this "mall' was actually the final incarnation of the infamous Luau Room that had evolved over the decades.

The Luau Room was built in the late 1960s, one of the many additions and renovations to the Palms complex. In 1964-65, New York hosted the World's Fair in Queens, boasting almost 140 pavilions—temporary structures

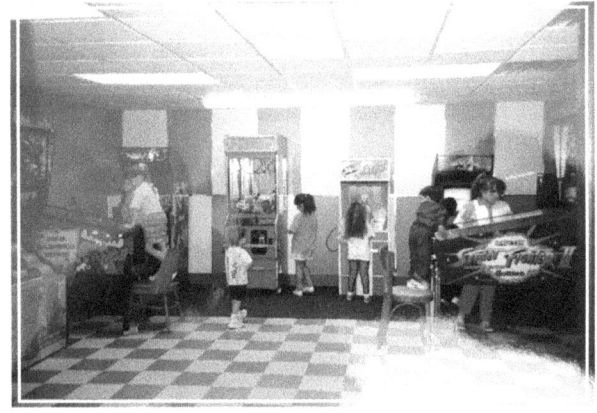

The arcade in the Luau Room mini mall in the 1990s

showcasing exhibits from different countries and states. After the Fair closed, newspapers advertised offers to buy those pavilions, allowing people to salvage construction materials, furniture, and decor before they were scrapped. Ever the opportunist, Grandpa

Bob jumped at the chance to buy a pavilion. He and a crew disassembled the structure, taking the steel beams, window frames, and other materials and used them to construct the Luau Room in the center of the Palms, so named for the Hawaiian-themed decorations adorning the new event space. Just like that, the Palms Shore Club owned a piece of the World's Fair.

When it opened in 1970, the Luau Room became an additional venue for parties, complete with its own kitchen, and my dad's friend Alan Horowitz as Maître D'—a separate option for weddings or events when the Palms and Rattan Rooms were booked. Unfortunately, Grandpa Bob didn't like to invest in new equipment and refused to stock the separate space. Instead, the waiters and busboys had to carefully haul heavy plates, glasses, tables and chairs back and forth—down the stairs, out of the main hall, and across the Palms grounds—before and after each party.

Never one to waste space, Grandpa Bob turned the flat roof of the building into another sundeck overlooking the pools, officially designated for card games on weekends and unofficially used as a hideout for cabana boys on break.

The space truly came to life in the late 1970s. *Saturday Night Fever* had just come out—filmed at the popular 2001 Odyssey disco club in Bay Ridge—and disco fever was overtaking Brooklyn. My dad, Allen, only twenty at the time, came up with one of his big ideas: turning the Luau Room into a disco. Grandpa Bob gave his blessing, and suggested the name: "Disco Hideaway". With a name, and a $500 disco ball, they were ready. My dad and two close friends, Ronald Kestenbaum and Alan Horowitz, launched the themed dance-party nights. My dad managed the bar and business; Alan took care of the front door, loosely checking IDs and collecting the entry fees from the young adults. And they poured in. With the drinking age still eighteen, everyone wanted to show off their John Travolta moves beneath the pulsing lights of the disco ball, drink in hand.

For a while, Disco Hideaway was a roaring success – a clever way to plug into the trends of the day to keep the Palms bustling during the off-season. Jeff Siber, just eighteen at the time, would spin the biggest hits as he launched his first DJ gigs under his new business, Jeffrey Craig. The Luau Room was packed with excited bodies, lines snaking out the door. My dad and his friends excitedly raised the entry fee from two to five dollars. But even with the price hike, the crowd kept coming. Then trouble came: too many people, too many drinks, and too many wannabe mobsters acting like they owned the place, puffing up their egos and demanding respect, sometimes physically. The young bartenders, some barely old enough to drink themselves, got a crash course in crowd control and diplomacy, learning how to calm the tough guys who leaned across the bar with a menacing, "You better take care of me."

Uncle Larry working at the Luau Room Snack Bar in the late 1970s (courtesy of Cindy Solomon)

Despite their best efforts, fights began breaking out almost nightly. Fists flew, chairs toppled, chaos reigned, and cleanup was constant. Eric Yorke remembers abandoning his post at the bar for a few minutes to help break up a fight, only to return and find the register empty. Whether a set-up or someone taking advantage of the distraction, it became a life lesson for Eric – always guard the cash! – and a warning bell for Disco Hideaway.

Bouncers were brought in, usually young, tough-looking guys from the Palms community, like Lee Stern and Glenn Guerriero, hired because they knew many regulars. They flexed their muscles, broke up escalating scuffles, and tried to keep the peace between hot-headed customers. But even they couldn't fully control the growing chaos. Grandpa Bob worried the disco might be shut down, or worse, lose its liquor license. By the second year, he decided to put an end to it himself. It was a short but unforgettable chapter in the life of the Luau Room.

Without a dedicated purpose, but in such a central location, the Luau Room continued to evolve. In the 1980s, it housed the third iteration of the ever-moving snack bar, run by Uncle Larry with his wife, my Aunt Joy, often manning the register. The Luau Room turned into a cabana-club hangout, filled with tables and several arcade games – and even a few casino machines like Joker Poker (which actually paid out!), supplied by Jimmy K and Dennis D, long-term cabana members and friends of Grandpa Bob. During the video game boom, being able to play *Popeye* or *Stargate* or *Punchout!* was a huge attraction for Palms teenagers. Of course, it required a lot of quarters, so they found ways to game the system. Some kicked the machines hard enough to trigger free credits; others discovered certain games like *Popeye* would register nickels as quarters. It was whispered about as a brilliant hack – until the time came to empty the machine and Grandpa Bob found the pile of offending nickels. After a few choice curse words, the *Popeye* machine was removed.

In the late 1990s, the snack bar moved out to the marina, and the Luau Room transformed into the "mini-mall" I would come to know well. A separate arcade room was walled off around the existing games, adding new favorites like *Street Fighter II*, *NBA Jam* and *Heavy Barrel*. The rest of the space filled with rotating businesses: a boutique managed by longtime cabana club member Shirley Lang; a nail salon where Grandma Gloria would take my cousins for special mani-pedis; a small gym with exercise machines for the few members so inclined; and a sundries shop run by Aunt Joy, selling snacks and summer trinkets. There were few traces of the original Luau Room left, but the space carried its layered history—decades of reinvented at the heart of the Palms Shore Club.

The Berfonds Move In

I remember slowly making my way up the concrete steps that led to my grandparents' house, peering over the railing to watch the sky darken over the Palms Shore Club. It was always strange to see the place so empty and quiet and still in the dusk, after the chaos and crowds of a summer day; in that twilight, it somehow looked smaller. But I loved these evenings when I would sleep over at the Palms, an excuse to get time with Grandma Gloria and Grandpa Bob all to myself. After the last stragglers had abandoned their cabanas and everything had been locked up, I would make the very short commute with my grandparents up to their home. Sometimes we'd change and go out for dinner, picking one of their regular restaurants along Emmons Avenue; other times we'd just stay in, playing hours-long games of War at the kitchen table or watching TV on the black leather couch. I never felt so special as those moments, walking in and out of this home they had built, cleverly perched above, yet in the midst of the complex, truly the throne room of their kingdom.

Grandma Gloria and Grandpa Bob spent most of their time at the Palms Shore Club from day one. However, for the first two decades, they officially lived with their sons in rented apartments nearby – initially at Nostrand Avenue and Avenue S, which required a short commute by car, later moving to Bedford Avenue, just a ten-minute walk away from the Palms.

My grandparents house in the back, overlooking the pools, rows of cabanas, and Sheepshead Bay

In the late 1970s, their living situation changed. Apparently, Grandma and Grandpa "forgot" to pay their rent and were not-so-politely asked to vacate their apartment. Alerted by their neighbor when the sheriff arrived one day, the family scrambled to find a truck, piled all their furniture in, and immediately moved out. Whether by accident or design, the situation created an opportunity: why not build their own home right on the Palms property? It would eliminate their commute after the long workdays, allow them to keep a watchful eye on everything, and perhaps most appealing, remove the need to owe anyone else money (a situation my grandparents did not love).

During the off-season, construction began on a single-story home built atop the flat concrete roof of the Luau Room, which had previously served as an extra sundeck. The family stayed in a Staten Island hotel in the meantime.

In 1979, the family moved into their completed brick home, along with their sweet husky, August. It was a comfortable house, with four bedrooms, living spaces, and a (rarely used) kitchen, all easily accessible via a staircase from the upper pool deck. From every window, the views were perfect—across the pools and into the event hall, and out toward the back patios and marina. A large terrace overlooked it all, a spot where you could quietly watch the Palms' evening events or the comings and goings of boats in the Bay. Adjacent to the terrace were the roofs of the Patio West cabanas, a convenient space for the dog to roam (and perhaps do his business). The building became a part of the Palms' landscape, a literal and symbolic extension of the Berfonds' reign. The family came and went over the years. Grandma Gloria's mother, my great-grandma Sadie, had her own room for a time. As my dad and his brothers grew older, they gradually moved out – to college and law school for Uncle Mel, to marriages and families of their own, to houses in Staten Island, New Jersey and Bay Ridge. In the early 1990s, my grandparents bought a beautiful house in Florida, where they spent the cold winter months like other New York "snowbirds". But the Palms home always remained the base for the family — the summer house, the place for visitors, the refuge to crash after long days or nights at the club.

A Rocky Relationship with the Neighborhood

My memories of Emmons Avenue centered around food. There was, of course, Roll-n-Roaster, just a short stroll down the road, our easy go-to when my sister and I were sun-weary after a day in the pool. My favorite was the chicken tenders and fries with cheese; my young palette hadn't yet developed an interest in their famous roast beef sandwiches.

Then there was Maria's, the family-favorite Italian spot across the avenue from the Palms. It was often my grandparents' choice when I stayed overnight with them. After closing, the three of us would make the quick walk over. I always felt special when the staff greeted my grandparents by name and brought out their usual orders.

My understanding of the neighborhood did not extend far beyond those favorite places, and it seemed a quiet backdrop as we drove up to the Palms. But that calm, steady environment belied a much more complicated and sometimes uneasy relationship between the Palms Shore Club and the main strip of Sheepshead Bay.

When the Palms Shore Club opened in the 1960s, it stood as a marker of progress for Sheepshead Bay, a shiny new attraction

Roll-n-Roaster, my favorite neighborhood restaurant, at its grand opening in 1971

meant to draw people to the waterfront year-round. But the reality was a bit more complicated. By the 1970s, the once-celebrated addition to the community had some detractors, and tensions with the Palms' closest neighbors along Emmons Avenue become hard to ignore. To start, there was Grandpa Bob's never-ending ambitions to improve and expand the Palms Shore Club. The original footprint included a single row of sports courts along the western edge of the complex, bordering a cluster of single-story bungalows owned by local families. It was already quite the juxtaposition; this gleaming cabana club, a symbol of leisure and status, standing beside a row of older, modest homes.

Before long, Grandpa Bob began buying up the adjacent bungalows, one by one, adding more sports courts and a day camp area—though he did, to his credit, leave a pathway so non-members could still access the pier. Some neighbors were happy to take the buy-out, but others proved more stubborn, requiring persuasion and patience.

The second incarnation of Bernie's Bait & Tackle shop on Emmons Avenue, which had been Palms Shore Club's closest and longest neighbor

One, in particular, Sam Underberg, owned the bungalow closest to the marina, the final property Grandpa Bob needed to complete his expansion. Underberg held out for years, insisting on an easement so he could reach Emmons Avenue through the newly-built area. There were fights, and eventually lawsuits, but in the end, Grandpa Bob prevailed. His victory allowed him to relocate the snack bar to the prime waterfront spot, where Underberg's bungalow once stood.

Fortunately, not everything on Emmons Avenue became a target for Grandpa Bob's expansion plans. Bernie's Bait & Tackle, the neighborhood's go-to fishing shop, stood right next to the Palms Shore Club for decades. Even as Grandpa bought and built around the property, he maintained a warm relationship with Bernie Schwartz and his family, who even had their own private entrance into the Palms through the back of their store.

It wasn't until the 1990s that Grandpa Bob finally purchased the property, and only because the Schwartzes wanted to expand. Bernie's Bait & Tackle simply moved a few doors down on Emmons Avenue, where it still stands to this day.

Then there was the parking situation – or rather, the parking chaos, as the neighbors would have called it. From the start, the Palms Shore Club never had nearly enough dedicated parking for the flood of cabana members and evening guests. For a time, the club rented nearby empty lots for valet parking, but one by one they were bought up by developers as the neighborhood evolved.

The young men who worked as valets did their best to manage the situation. Some were dependable, like John Truisi, one of the trusted attendants in the '80s, whose mechanic skills came in handy whenever a guest's car wouldn't start. Others, though, some barely old enough to have their driver's license, were a bit more fast and loose in their methods, sometimes taking the 'scenic route' to find a parking spot or adding an extra mile or two on the nicer cars' odometers.

In later years, Grandpa Bob managed to carve out a small parking lot beside the property, but it never came close to meeting demand. The shortage became a real issue when he tried to turn the snack bar by the marina into a full-fledged public restaurant overlooking the bay. The city shut down the plan, citing insufficient designated parking. Beyond derailing another classic Bob Berfond business idea, the parking problem remained an ongoing source of friction. Palms guests filled every public space along Emmons Avenue, double-parked, blocked traffic, and generally made life difficult for neighboring businesses and families.

So, it wasn't exactly surprising when those simmering tensions occasionally boiled over. One such incident happened in the late 1970s, when my dad, ever the entrepreneur, decided to make his own mark by starting a *moped* rental business with his friend Ronald Kestenbaum. They set up shop in front of the Palms, and for the first few weeks, things went smoothly. Until one afternoon, when a dispute broke out with a neighborhood guy, apparently over a damaged moped and an unpaid fee.

Within minutes, his friends appeared—a pack of well-built local boys in the stereotypical white sleeveless undershirts, 'wifebeater' tank tops—flexing and posturing in the middle of Emmons Avenue, baiting my dad and his friends. Words quickly turned to shoves, shoves to punches, and soon a full-blown brawl erupted in the street. The police arrived and the chaos had scattered, leaving only bruised faces, a failed business venture, and heightened animosity that had to be resolved by the elders behind closed doors. There were no real winners, just a few more scars in the long, uneasy relationship between the Palms and its neighbors.

There were times when the Palms became swept up in neighborhood chaos, like the day a hostage crisis unfolded in one of the small bungalows next door to the club. It was a typical summer afternoon in the early 1990s: the pool was busy, the music was loud, and kids were running around the camp, when suddenly the sharp crack of gunfire tore through the day. Within seconds, people were jumping out of the pool, shouting, running for cover. The counselors quickly gathered the children in the day camp and lined them up against the wall, trying to keep everyone calm.

Soon a SWAT team arrived, and the Palms was put on lockdown. No one was allowed on the east side of the complex. In a bungalow adjacent to the paddleball courts, a recently released ex-convict was holding his former wife and daughter hostage at gunpoint. Snipers took positions on the roofs of the cabanas and the catering hall, scanning the bungalow below for any sign of movement and ready to take action. The crowd waited anxiously.

It wasn't until late that night that the situation was diffused, with everyone miraculously unharmed. The scared and exhausted children were finally released from the camp area, and everyone was able to go home, shaken but safe. It became one of those stories those at the Palms remembered for years, but one that no one ever wanted to live through again.

A Spin-Off: The Palms Country Club

Our family wasn't one for road trips. But it was hard to resist the temptation to take a slight a detour and steep ourselves in a bit of Berfond history. My parents had just picked up my sister and me from our sleepaway camp in Upstate New York when they realized we weren't far from South Fallsburg in the Catskills, once home to the Palms Country Club.

We drove through the quiet, desolate area and pulled up to what had once been the entrance, now marked only by a weathered sign and a rusted chain, which my mom moved aside. I was probably eight or nine at the time and hadn't even known there had been another Palms venue before that day. I remember walking stoically through the eerie, overgrown grounds, the abandoned buildings sagging with age—my dad silent, my mom with tears in her eyes.

Through the weeds, my sister spotted a piece of paper and bent down to pick it up. It was a brochure, faded but intact, depicting the grandeur and promise of the new Palms Country Club, an extension of the Palms summer brand and, once upon a time, the perfect site for a future casino.

Grandpa Bob was the type to seize any opportunity he saw, as evidenced by the Palms Shore Club itself. Through the 1960s, he had kept up parts of his construction business, building a handful of single- and multi-family homes in Brighton Beach. But what he was really doing was waiting, biding his time until he could rebuild the empire he and his brother had started.

So in the early 1970s, when he began hearing rumblings about a new gambling mecca on the East Coast, his interest was piqued. The rumored contenders for legalized gambling were the Catskills in Upstate New York, the Poconos in Pennsylvania, and, of course, Atlantic City in New Jersey.

Perhaps unsurprisingly, given his risk tolerance, Grandpa Bob was himself a gambler. His idea of family time was taking Grandma Gloria and the kids to the racetrack on Monday evenings, their one regular night out, where he could teach his sons how to place bets. To him, the Catskills looked like a solid wager.

The "Borscht Belt", as it was known, was already a favorite summer destination for New York's Jewish families, later immortalized in *Dirty Dancing* and *The Marvelous Mrs. Maisel*. Grandpa had seen its heyday in the 1960s, when hundreds of resorts overflowed with families who drove the two or three hours north to immerse themselves in a self-contained world of food, entertainment, and leisure. It was a world Grandpa Bob understood instinctively from the Palms Shore Club, and he gambled that an early investment there, before any official casino approvals came through, might just be his next big win.

In late 1970, Grandpa Bob, his cousin, Bernie and business partner Morris Berkowitz purchased a rundown old resort in Fallsburg, Sullivan County. The Eldorado Hotel (formerly Hotel Zeiger) had been one of the largest and most popular destinations in the

Photo of the abandoned Palms Shore Club property in the early 2000s, where you can still see the P-A-L-M-S lettering on the arched facade

Catskills during its 1960s peak. After closing in 1967, the property had been repurposed as a dormitory for students at Sullivan County Community College.

A Spin-Off: The Palms Country Club

But Grandpa saw another life in the old hotel. Over the next several months, his team poured in time, sweat, and a small fortune, and sweat, gutting and restoring the property to its former grandeur,

building it up to even more extravagance. Rafael, the Palms handyman, along with several other men who worked for Grandpa Bob, was sent Upstate for the winter to handle the renovations, essentially living in the hotel's construction zone. They ripped out and burned old materials to make room for the new, transforming the place piece by piece.

Photo of the abandoned Palms Shore Club property in the early 2000s, where you can still see the impressive four-sided fireplace in the lobby

They redid the lobby with a beautiful, four-sided fireplace, upgraded the nightclub and existing large swimming pool, put in a switchboard and operators, and connected several stand-alone outbuildings to construct amenities that were unimaginable at that time – an indoor pool, a sauna, an ice-skating rink. By 1971, the once-forgotten property in Fallsburg reopened as the impressive Palms Country Club.

Picture the resort at its height. During the day, families and friends lounged in chaises by the pool, played softball and tennis and shuffleboard. Children were occupied and happy in day camp

A Spin-Off: The Palms Country Club

programs, running on the playground, doing arts and crafts and making fast friends.

Canarsie Courrier article about the extravagant "This is Your Life" tribute event for Meade Esposito bringing hundreds of New York elite to the Palms Country Club in 1972

The Palms Shore Club

In the evening, couples traded their bathing suits for dresses and slacks, gathering in the dining hall for lavish dinners followed by entertainment – rising comedians, live musicians, and all-night dancing – while babysitters kept watch over the kids. As with the Palms Shore Club, the Country Club also became a magnet for politicians and their celebrations. Most notably, in May 1972, it hosted an elaborate *This Is Your Life*-style tribute to Brooklyn Democratic leader Meade Esposito. Several hundred guests – including a who's who of New York legislators, judges, and other political luminaries – journeyed all the way to Fallsburg, packing the resort for an evening of good-natured gags, warm toasts and affectionate memories.

And the fun wasn't just for the guests – the staff had a grand old time too. Grandpa Bob, of course, couldn't be in two places at once, so the Country Club was managed day-to-day by Palms' stalwart, Frankie Cass. Grandpa also called on his younger cousin Andy who, in true Palms' tradition, had been studying hotel and restaurant management at Sullivan County Community College – and had actually lived in the hotel when it served as a dorm. Grandpa asked Andy to take on the role of dining manager, stewarding and supplying the kitchen and dining room for the all-important resort meals.

Several of the Palms "family" were sent to Upstate to join Frankie and Andy, including Seymour, Mike Wind, and Grandpa Bob's sister Sheila and her daughter Arlyn. Friends who had been working at other hotels in the region were brought in as waiters and busboys. Many were in their late teens or early twenties, and for them, it was essentially like sleepaway camp with a paycheck.

They worked hard, keeping the guests happy, serving endless trays of food and drinks. Three meals a day was a marathon: by the time breakfast cleanup was done, guests were already lining up for lunch, and so on. Both the girls and boys had to tie back their long 1970s hairdos for service—one waiter, Bobby, even opted to wear a wig instead. But after hours, they had the freedom to visit other hotels in the area or simply stay up all night together, finding their own amusement the way young people in the 1970s did.

For Andy, the parties extended beyond the summer. At Grandpa Bob's request, when everyone else packed to head back to Brooklyn, Andy stayed behind to live in the empty resort for the rest of the year, keeping an eye on things and helping with maintenance. Sometimes he would invite friends for the weekend and blast music through the cavernous, empty halls from his sound system, reveling in his unique 'hotel-sitting' job. He just had to make sure everything was tidied up for the weekly check-ins, when Grandpa Bob would send someone from Brooklyn to act as the real adult in the room.

While my grandparents weren't there full time, they regularly visited during the summer season. To celebrate my Uncle Mel's bar mitzvah, they took all of his friends up to the Palms Country Club for the weekend, hiring a bus to shuttle the group to the Catskills. My dad, an industrious fifteen-year old at the time, brought along a miniature craps table to keep everyone entertained on the drive. By the time they arrived at the hotel, he had taken his brothers' friends for all they had.

Despite the fun times it provided, the Palms Country Club struggled financially. The grounds and amenities, while extremely impressive, were equally expensive to maintain—three meals a day, nightly shows, and the upkeep of the pools and premises throughout the year. Even with a hundred rooms booked all summer, the income was not enough to keep pace with the costs. They tried to expand, building another wing of guest rooms, but even that proved unsustainable. The summer season was too short, and in the off-season, the resort was poorly equipped to host guests—half the rooms had no heat. It became a sore spot between Grandpa Bob and his cousin Bernie, who couldn't understand why they hadn't invested in a proper heating system for a hotel in the mountains. The arguments over the heat—and the growing tension between the cousins over the resort's future—eventually led to their falling out.

The best hope was a fully booked summer season, but even that was becoming rare across the Borscht Belt. After its peak in the 1960s, the region began to decline in popularity in the 1970s, as Jewish families found it easier and more affordable to travel farther afield by train or plane. The long-anticipated legalization of gambling in the Catskills never materialized, a major blow to Grandpa Bob's plans. Despite strong lobbying from those who believed casinos could revive the resort economy, the efforts were voted down. Instead, in 1977, Atlantic City became the first U.S. city outside Nevada to legalize casino gambling, drawing away the very audience the Catskills once served. Resorts across the region began shutting their doors, and in 1972, after just its second summer season, the Palms Country Club, still shiny and new, followed suit. With the area in decline, there were no ready buyers, and much of the property remains as it was, but now overgrown and in disrepair. A vestige of a brilliant vision, but ultimately a gamble that didn't pay off: a short-lived spin-off of the Palms legacy, and one small chapter in the rise and fall of the Borscht Belt.

The Catering Era I: Every Affair is a Palms Affair

THE CHANGING TIMES OF THE 1980s AND 1990s

Boy, did our family know how to party! With the Palms Shore Club at our disposal, there was no reason not to turn every occasion into a huge celebration. I have vague memories of the similarly extravagant "1, 2, 3" birthday party: I had just turned three, my cousin Jake was two, and my cousin Lindsey one, our birthdays all within a month, the perfect opportunity for a joint Berfond grandchildren celebration. This one had many more children running around, and to entertain us all, our parents pulled out every party trick in the Palms book — face painting, balloon animals, and entertainers juggling and dressed up as characters. My memory is more distinct for my sister's bat mitzvah: the room gleaming with magenta and teal balloons and decorations; dozens of thirteen-year-olds bussed in from New Jersey, led by a police escort to guide them through the Verrazano Bridge traffic; all of the best Palms menu items on display. It always felt so special, but I now understand that us Berfonds weren't the only family to celebrate all of our milestones at the Palms.

By the 1980s, my dad, Allen, along with his brother Larry, had stepped in as full-time managers of the catering business, which had become the main focus in the Palms' three-story hall. In earlier decades, those rooms were mostly used for public dining, dancing and entertainment, with only the occasional large wedding, bar mitzvah, prom, or charity gala taking over a full room.

My dad, Allen, in the 1990s, in his domain -- the lobby area of the Palms catering hall

Yet, there was clearly a larger market in Brooklyn for fully private events – especially at a venue that boasted sweeping views of Sheepshead Bay. In the 1970s, Neil Kasman, then a partner in the event hall, and later Julie Erlich, began booking more and more of these parties. In the afternoons, they would set up round tables for bar mitzvahs and weddings, and once the horahs were danced and the mazel tovs shouted, young waiters like Kenny Mollins and Elliot Eskenazi – under the supervision of the professionals Marty and Benny – would clear the guests out to quickly flip the room for the nightclub crowd.

Reliable Louie Rodriguez, the legendary dishwasher and cleaner, would do a tour-de-force sweep of the room in forty minutes flat, while the waiters and bus-boys swapped back in the long rectangular tables.

By the 1980s, the balance had shifted -- with the popularity of the nightclub format gradually declining and the catered affairs picking up. Over the years, a series of renovations had created a beautiful venue for all manner of events: weddings, bat and bar mitzvahs, and Sweet Sixteens, but also anniversaries, engagement parties, surprise birthdays, bridal showers, high-school proms and reunions. Guests now included New Yorkers far beyond the original cabana club membership.

The upstairs Palms Room was able to accommodate around 300 guests, while the main-floor Imperial Room, formerly the Rattan Room of the 1960s, held about 100 once the large bar was removed. Downstairs, the space that had once housed the beloved snack bar was converted into a chapel, perfect for on-site wedding ceremonies and bar or bat mitzvah services. The chapel was always adorned with fresh flowers, courtesy of the Palms' regular florist, Mike "Wrecker" Andriano – who had his own small refrigerated workspace adjacent to the room, where he crafted his arrangements with a cigar perpetually hanging from his mouth. Between these three event rooms, and the flexible outdoor spaces that came alive on summer evenings, the Palms was a perfect venue for any occasion. By the 1980s and 1990s, almost everyone in Sheepshead Bay had either attended or hosted a private celebration there. Families often returned again and again, hosting second, third, even fourth milestones under the Palms' roof, spanning generations of weddings, bar mitzvahs, birthdays and anniversaries.

Wedding setup in the Palm Room in the 1990s

The steady stream of guests was a testament to the Palms Shore Club's reputation for high quality service. At the core was the food – always abundant and consistently delicious– dished up by the longtime kitchen crew. Every event began with colorful, beautifully arranged cold platters, including elaborate fruit displays carved by the dedicated *garde manger*. Cocktail hours featured silver trays piled high with hors d'oeuvres, followed by buffet dinners with chafing dishes, carving stations, and sumptuous hot entrees, or, for formal affairs, elegant sit-down service in the classic French style.

Guests milling around the pool for an even outdoor cocktail hour in the 1990s

In the 1990s, the Palms added a new attraction: a sushi bar staffed by two Japanese chefs who prepared fresh rolls and artful displays, a surprising but popular addition. And then came the finale: the Palms' famous Viennese table. Carts rolled out from the kitchen laden with a dazzling array of cakes, pastries, and chocolate covered strawberries, often followed by a candy wagon overflowing with treats from Williams Candy, a Coney Island institution and Palms partner since its earliest days. The moment the wagon appeared, it was instantly mobbed by kids of every age. No other venue's dessert table could compare.

Occasionally, when the hosts knew their guests would want to party all night, they would even plan for breakfast to be served at 2 a.m. or so, to soak up the alcohol that had likely been fueling the endless dancing and fun.

Then there was the entertainment. The regular house DJ, Jeff Siber, known professionally as 'Jeffrey Craig', knew exactly how to get a party going, spinning the favorites of the day and hyping up the crowd. Working at the Palms was his big break. Jeff was a friend of my dad from high-school, and barely out of his teens when he began playing the growing number of catered events in the mid-to-late 1970s. Over more than two decades at the Palms, he built both his business and a rolodex of connections, soon booking private parties at other venues, including for some of the Palms' more notorious guests. It was there that he honed the skills and relationships that later led to his partnership in Total Entertainment, a multi-million-dollar enterprise based in New Jersey.

For those guests who preferred live music, there were the bands – often the lively sounds of Joey Dale's band in the earlier years, or Prime Time in the later ones, both guaranteed to bring guests to their feet.

And the fun wasn't limited to those with invitations. Some events remained open to the public. During Passover, for instance, the Palms hosted community seders where families from the cabana club and beyond could gather to celebrate. With a seat set aside for Elijah, a rabbi and cantor would lead the seder while the packed room was served multiple courses of kosher-style food, from matzo ball soup to stuffed cabbage to chocolate macaroons. On the other end of the spectrum, much less family-friendly – were the dedicated ladies' nights and men's nights, where food, drinks and music were complemented by the more risqué entertainment of male dancers (for the former) and female strippers (for the latter).

Most popular of all was the annual New Year's Eve extravaganza. The hall would be decked out with shimmering streamers (a small miracle they survived, given all of the smoking of the era), champagne was plentiful, and guests in gowns and tuxedos crowded in for the night. With so many cabana members in attendance, and staff who knew them well, it was, in essence, a Palms-extended-family celebration: a late, wild night of drinking, dancing, and toasting, and some of the most memorable New Year's Eves for guests and workers alike.

One New Year's Eve in the late 1980s was particularly memorable, because the final guests to arrive were the cops. The Palms had been overflowing with partygoers on all three floors, likely nearly five hundred revelers in total. As the night wound down, everyone surged toward the same coat check room at once. In the drunken chaos, a few hot-headed men exchanged words, and before anyone could intervene, the argument snowballed into a thirty-on-thirty brawl. The police eventually broke it up and sent everyone home, a memorable start to the New Year.

That was hardly the only fight in the Palms' long, colorful history, perhaps not surprising, given the Brooklyn machismo (or as we might now call it, toxic masculinity) of the time. One altercation ended with a trail of shattered mirrors. It happened during a rather dramatic wedding, where recent infidelity by the groom led many of the bride's guests to stay away. The couple still went through with their vows in a half-empty room, but the celebration turned violent when the groom and his father-in-law came to blows near the mirrored bathrooms.

On a different night, the fall-out was between two separate wedding parties. No one could say how it started, a few words exchanged between guests from the third-floor Palms Room and the second-floor Imperial Room, perhaps. But it ended with both parties pouring into the street as onlookers gathered to watch an all-out brawl. Once again, the Brooklyn police arrived to restore order, another unforgettable evening at the Palms.

Fortunately, my grandparents and dad were on good terms with the local precincts, whose officers were summoned many times to break up fights at the Palms. Some even stopped by when they were off-the-clock, for their own celebrations. In 1993, NYPD Detective Bill Clark hosted a premiere party at the Palms for what would become the beloved, award-winning police drama *NYPD Blue*. Detective Clark, whose real-life cases inspired many of the show's storylines, served as both technical consultant and, eventually, as an executive producer. For the series premiere, he invited scores of his NYPD colleagues to watch the episode on multiple screens set up throughout the venue.

There were also plenty of precinct parties over the years – usually heavy on drinking, and once even ending in their own brawl that ended with guns drawn.

On the milder end of lawlessness was the regular petty theft by guests at the Palms Shore Club. Over time, the staff noticed cloth napkins and silverware slowly disappearing. But some thieves were more brazen. Busboy Anthony Scire, now known to Z100 listeners as Skeery Jones, remembers working one wedding in the early 1990s. When Donna Summer's "Last Dance"—always the final song of the evening—started playing, he went to clear the last table, and noticed that all of the new, expensive black-stemmed water glasses were gone.

Moments later, as the last guests were leaving, my dad spotted a woman holding two oversized plastic bags with suspiciously clanking contents inside. A quick investigation revealed a dozen of the missing glasses – and a puddle of water beneath the table, where she had emptied them before slipping them into her bags, apparently thinking no one would notice.

There was rarely a boring night at the Palms Shore Club.

But, fortunately, it wasn't only the chaos—violence and theft included—that made the Palms so memorable. The food, the staff, the atmosphere, and the sheer joy of celebration kept families coming back again and again, across multiple generations. The repeat gatherings didn't just grow the Palms' business, they deepened the community connection, turning the venue into a true neighborhood institution.

The Catering Era II: Allen & His Crew

Fold the napkin in quarters, then diagonally. Tuck under the two corners carefully, and turn it over to make sure the cloth napkin resembled a little house. Another one done! This was probably the hardest I ever concentrated at seven years old— sitting alone at one of the half-set round tables in the Imperial Room, with a pile of cloth napkins in the celebrants' chosen hue at my left and a stack of folded creations at my right.

All around me, several Palms staff were busy preparing the room for that evening's event – including my dad, who checked on me regularly and praised my work. I never felt prouder than when I could tell him I had completed all the napkins or finished setting the utensils around the tables, my other regular task. I was so excited to be a small part of my dad's incredible catering crew.

Through most of the 1980s and 1990s, my dad, Allen, oversaw the Palms' catering business – the parties, the events, and even the fights – often peering down from the glass windows of his office, perched a half-floor above the Imperial Room in the lobby. He was only in his mid-twenties when he began taking on the role, but he quickly earned his father's trust and the autonomy to run the place, with my Uncle Larry by his side managing the events themselves.

Whether learned from my grandparents or simply innate, my dad had a sharp business instinct that everyone respected. He carried the authority and confidence needed to handle the endless demands of the job—booking parties, planning entertainment, and overseeing each event to ensure it met the family's high standards. He was always attentive to the customers' needs and experiences, doing whatever it took to make sure they wanted to come back, and to uphold the Palms' proud reputation.

The Catering Era II: Allen & His Crew

The crew lined up and ready to serve buffet style in the 1990s

Perhaps the most demanding part of my dad's job was managing the staff — some senior waiters, but mostly a young crew of servers, cocktail waitresses, bartenders, and busboys. My dad was stern but fair, known for being good to his employees: caring, generous and intensely loyal. In his early years of management, he did adopt his father's penchant for yelling, though it generally didn't carry quite the same weight without Grandpa Bob's imposing stare and formidable presence.

Under my dad's and Uncle Larry's supervision, the staff was generally attentive and hard-working, even though the job wasn't easy. For many, it was their first position, or they had graduated from the more relaxed cabana club summer gigs — so there was plenty of learning on the job. The days were long, filled with hours of set-up, service and cleanup, and the added pressure of quickly turning over rooms when multiple events were scheduled back-to-back. It was on one of those especially hectic days when my dad's temper rose to match Grandpa Bob's. The photographers from an afternoon party were taking too long to pack up, ignoring repeated requests to clear the room. Finally, my dad lost his patience, grabbed their equipment, and flung it unceremoniously down the stairs leading to the main entrance. The photographers were furious about their mangled cameras, but Dad quickly moved on to preparing for the next event.

Then there were the unnecessary burdens. Grandpa Bob refused to purchase enough tables and chairs, so the staff had to lug the heavy furniture up and down the stairs – carrying chairs from the first-floor chapel to the third-floor Palm Room while wedding guests enjoyed a cocktail hour on the second floor. Then there were the large air conditioning units, which Grandpa Bob refused to invest in maintaining. They would constantly break down, making the long hours sweatier and more arduous for the staff.

One summer in the early 1980s, all of the main A.C. units failed at the same time. Even after buying a few small interim units, the stuffy heat was unbearable. In a moment of desperation, Grandpa

Maitre d Stevie Efron (at right) with the crew, serving French-style service in the 1990s

decided to break several of the large, beautiful glass windows, just to let in a bit of air—a risky move, since they had to ensure no one accidentally fell into the pools below. Still, that summer became legendary: the staff running themselves ragged in the sweltering heat, bringing endless pitchers of water to overheated guests; brides with hair wilting and makeup melting; groomsmen loosening their ties and shedding jackets in surrender.

These experiences certainly built the work ethic and the resilience – not to mention the muscles – of the young staff. Many gained skills that stayed with them for life. Several still credit the Palms for their turkey carving expertise, having spent countless hours behind the carving stations; to this day, they're the go-to family members at Thanksgiving.

But with all of that hard work, the staff also wanted to have fun – and sometimes my dad's yelling was fully warranted. The catering hall crew was practically one big family, a lively group of teens and twenty-somethings who worked hard and played harder.

Stevie Efron, the long-time maitre d' and a close friend of my dad and Uncle Larry, once pulled an unforgettable prank on the staff and even customers. The state lottery jackpot that Saturday was sky-high, and Stevie convinced the whole crew to chip in for a few tickets. When he bounded in the next morning, he was practically shouting that they had won! He showed them the ticket and even had them call the lottery hotline to confirm those were the winning numbers. Everyone was ecstatic, barely able to focus on working the day's event, as they shared their excitement with the customers. But later that evening, Stevie burst the bubble. Grinning, he held up the ticket again and pointed to the fine print: it was dated Sunday. He had bought it that morning, using the previous day's winning numbers. There was some good-natured grumbling, but in the end, it was just another bit of mischief in a long line of hijinks.

Funny Mike Kuller – known as "King" for his larger-than-life presence – was infamous for his pranks, most often aimed at my father, while being egged on by his brother Evan. Then there was Billy Vitolo, the bartender with a knack for mixing experimental cocktails, and testing out his creations on the cocktail waitresses. Letitia Yemma, Faith Cohen, Lisa Rayden, Suzanne Lee, and Annika Kaye were frequently his (very willing) guinea pigs. Naturally, that sometimes meant the waitresses got a little tipsy while making their rounds. That was a bridge too far for my dad. He finally put his foot down: no drinking until dessert was served. Fair enough. Billy quickly adapted. As soon as dessert went out, he'd line up shots for the crew like clockwork. The busboys, waiters and other bartenders would join, a rotating roster that included Kevin Barsky, Neal Israel, Rafael Lopez, Joe "Savage" Puorro, Perry Rausher, Andy Rubin and, unrelated, brothers Joel and Matt Rubin, as well as several others. With some sustenance in their system, they'd goof off while closing down, firing soda guns and launching leftover ice buckets at each other.

Then it was time to head out for more drinking and fun – usually to local bars like Captain Walter's, Christopher's, or Wheelers, or even the Sheepshead Bay Diner. It was on one of those nights at Wheelers when my Uncle Larry met his future wife Joy Goldberg.

Other romances and flings blossomed between the staff, as you'd expect from people spending so much time together. While most of it happened off premises, a few couples were caught together in the bridal room.

Even if they were scheduled to work the next day, the 2 p.m. start time left plenty of time to stay out all night, sleep until noon, and do it all over again. A few times, the after party was slightly further away – namely, Atlantic City. Uncle Larry even rented a bus. The staff, still in their black and white uniforms, piled in for the two-hour ride down to the Trump Taj Mahal. After a quick nap on the way down, they were ready to drink and gamble the night away.

Letitia Yemma, one of the cocktail waitresses, remembers joining these evenings out with her friend, Faith Cohen, even when they were no longer working at the Palms. They'd hang out in my dad's office, waiting for the parties to wrap up, and then tag along with their friends who were still on the clock for the usual post-shift fun. My dad would join the after-party now and then, and when he did, everyone relaxed — their wallets were safe. He was (and still is) the kind of guy who buys drinks for the whole table — not just for his staff, but for their friends, and even for random bar patrons who said *hello*. Whether he knew them or not. Because in Sheepshead Bay, everyone knew Allen Berfond. And if someone asked why he was buying, he'd just shrug as he sent over a drink and say, "Hey — can't hurt to stay on their good side."

My dad, however, steered clear of the other recreational activities that were favorites among the young catering hall staff – like, unsurprisingly, smoking pot. A few of the guys would sneak off before parties started, hunting out secret spots for a quick smoke — sometimes a storage closet, other times the walk-in refrigerator or the bridal room (also a popular spot for bridal parties to indulge in the illicit substance of the day). One winter evening, a few of them went to get supplies from the snack bar, which was then located in the Luau Room. The building was quiet and dark in the off-season, a perfect spot for their fun. Just as they were about to light up, a different kind of light flickered on the other side of the room. There was Grandpa Bob, sitting alone in the snack bar, smoking his cigarette – not exactly thrilled to be interrupted, especially by on-the-clock employees partaking in illicit activities. Needless to say, the boys got in trouble, and after that, the snack bar was officially off limits.

Despite – or maybe partly because of – these shenanigans, the staff at the Palms were quite good at their jobs, friendly and professional. While people rotated in-and-out, it was a relatively close-knit crew under my dad's leadership, and it made some of the Berfond events even more memorable.

Take my dad's 30th birthday party in October 1987. Over 150 people gathered, partying late into the night to celebrate their friend – and for many, boss – affectionately known as 'Oopie.' I've been told the nickname came from my dad's lack of coordination playing sports with his buddies — though who knows if it has another origin.

The night had the usual mix of food, drinks, and dancing – including with the core five Berfond family showing off their moves in a circle of clapping guests. Several of the long-time staff members, mostly there as guests, even belted out a special song dedicated to my dad, who sat in the middle, flushed with embarrassment and some alcohol. Then the whole room broke into a rousing rendition of 'We Are Family'.

As the night went on, and after the children went home (including my sister, Jackie, who was just three years old at the time), the vibe became a bit more X-rated. Ladies danced and stripped in large cages, a surprise birthday "gift" from my Uncle Larry to his older brother.

My sister Jackie's elaborate 1st birthday party, with videographer and DJ Jeff Siber in the back.

This was just one of many over-the-top Berfond celebrations held at the Palms. For my sister Jackie's first birthday party in 1985, over a hundred adults had gathered in the Imperial Room to celebrate Bob and Gloria's first grandchild. Beyond the usual extravagances – like an enormous Big Bird cake and professional videographer – Grandpa Bob surprised the family by hiring a horse for the day. Not a pony, but a full-sized beautiful white horse that the toddlers could take turns riding alongside a row of cabanas. But perhaps the best part was the collective singing of Happy Birthday. While my sister understandably cried, the guests and all of the staff belted the lyrics with enthusiasm, celebrating the growing Berfond family — the next generation of Allen's crew.

A Berfond Wedding & Other Love Stories

It really was quite dreamy. Watching the bride and groom walk off of the stage, hand-in-hand, to the cheers of their guests— the summer sky darkening above, boats drifting slowly into the Bay behind them. From the terrace of my grandparents' house, I loved to watch these outdoor wedding ceremonies set on the Palms' back patio. I'd sweep away the broken seashells scattered across the deck, rudely dropped by the persistent seagulls who'd scooped their shellfish dinners from the Bay. Then I'd settle in, soaking up the sights and sounds of the evening celebrations. At the time, I didn't realize that this was the setting for perhaps the most notable celebration at the Palms Shore Club: my parents' wedding in 1981.

My mom, Barbie Goldman, was nineteen when she first stepped into the Palms Shore Club in February 1976. Her best friend at Brooklyn College, Barbara Reich Borrero, had been working there for about a year and was often charged with bringing in more girls to help out at key events. That night, Barbara had enlisted my mom to pitch in at the year's Festa Italiana – handing out little cups of wine and doing whatever else was needed. It was the first of many evenings my mom would spend working at the Palms, most often as a

The happy couple, Barbie and Allen

The Palms Shore Club

Cocktail hour photo where you can see the floating floral centerpieces, and in the back, my mom and her bridesmaids taking pictures through the hall window

cocktail waitress in the nightclub or a bartender outside in those early years. It was the perfect weekend job: just a fifteen-minute commute from her family apartment in Gravesend; decent pay to help support her through college; and the chance to work with her friend Barbara and a fun group of peers, including Rita Kirschenbaum Kestenbaum and Debbie Horowitz. All of which more than made up for the cigarette smoke that would cling to her black shirt and skirt uniform by the end of the night. Another perk? A handsome, smart boss named Allen, who treated his staff well – especially in making sure that the waitresses always got home safe after late nights.

For more than a year, my mom's and dad's relationship was strictly professional. But there was always a casual, family-like vibe among the Palms staff. So when my dad received birthday tickets to the short-lived Broadway musical *Beatlemania* in 1977, Grandma Gloria actually encouraged him to take one of the cocktail waitresses along. He chose to invite the cute brunette Barbie, just like that, the oldest Berfond son was officially taken.

A Berfond Wedding & Other Love Stories

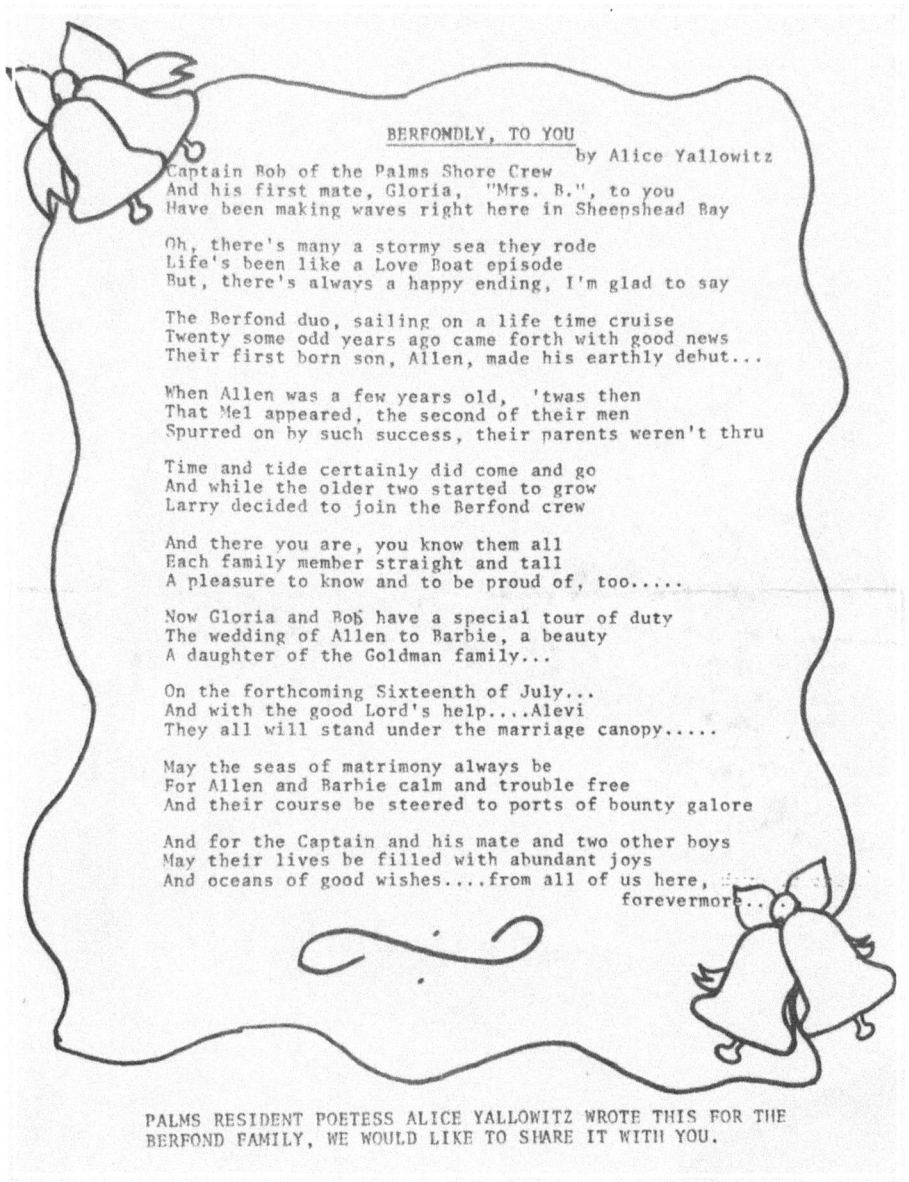

Poem in celebration of Barbie and Allen by cabana member and 'Palms resident poetess' Alice Yallowitz

The two were engaged in October 1980, and preparations began for the ultimate Palms Shore Club wedding. Of course, the date had to be chosen carefully to work around the Palms catering schedule and cabana club season, and to ensure the biggest VIPs in the

Berfond network would attend. After much consideration, the date was set: Thursday, July 16, 1981.

My dad and grandparents took the lead on planning, eager to pull out all of the stops and impress the long guest list. My mom focused on her must-haves: a lavender color theme, sterling silver roses woven in the floral arrangements, and, of course, her classic 80s white lace dress complete with a matching hat. The rest – the floral centerpieces, the cake, most of the guest list – was handled by the Berfond side. Every loyal vendor was asked to bring their A-game for the over 300 guests who would attend.

Beautiful wedding keepsake for my parents, with invitation transposed on photo from the 1981 wedding day, showing the cocktail hour - and in very back right - ceremony set-up

Though 300 guests was a sizable number, it was still a relatively limited list, as many in the Palms Shore Club community wanted to celebrate the nuptials, too. So, on Tuesday, July 14, a free dinner was offered to all cabana club members in honor of Barbie and Allen. This replaced the usual Wednesday Night Dinner, since the following evening would be reserved for wedding set up. It was an evening filled with the best Palms food, music and dancing, and plenty of well wishes for the happy couple.

But that was just a prelude. On Thursday, an absolutely perfect, cool summer evening, my parents said their "I dos" in an outdoor ceremony on the large back patio. They walked back down the aisle together as man and wife accompanied by a choir singing softly, while several white doves –some rather reluctantly– were released from cages perched atop flower-covered pillars lining both sides of the aisle.

Guests then made their way to an elaborate cocktail hour on the upper pool deck, floral centerpieces floating gracefully in the pool, and a band provided a lovely soundtrack from the cabana deck above. Afterwards everyone headed upstairs to the Palm Room for the reception– an evening filled with food, dancing, and drinking. For dessert, guests had the option to return outside by the pool– perhaps not the best idea, as one friend, Steven M, ended up taking an unexpected swim in the pool, a fitting end for a Palms celebration.

The wedding cemented my mom's place in the core Palms Shore Club cast. Like so many others, she began taking on a wider range of roles: cashier at the snack bar, seller of 'funny money' at Sunday night barbecues, and perhaps most unexpectedly, but excitingly, in-house party decorator. In the mid-1980s, when a construction company wanted centerpieces for a 'Knights of the Roundtable' themed event at the Palms, my mom took the leap. Flexing both her creative and quick-learning skills, she crafted knight figures holding swords– the first of many fun and impressive showpieces. She worked regularly with my dad in the Palms catering business, building the customized décor– the centerpieces and marquis signs, the balloon bouquets and arches– for many of the events he managed. It was a true partnership.

While the marriage of grandpa Bob's and grandma Gloria's oldest son was certainly a highlight, my parents' was not the only successful love story to bloom at the Palms. Some, however, got off to a rockier start. For example, the story of my dad's friend Stevie Efron in 1989. One day, while setting up for an event in the Palm Room, Stevie paused to look out the windows over the pool— a favorite pastime for the young men working in the catering hall, thanks to the clear view of the mostly female lifeguards at that time. It was then that Stevie spotted the pretty new lifeguard, Rory Staines, and decided he needed to make a move. Calling on his friend, Joel Rubin, another waiter, Stevie put together a tray with a flower in a vase and the now infamous poem that would live on in Palms lore: *"I wish I was a bar of soap, so clean, white and mushy; So every time you take a bath, I could swim around your tushy."*

Joel delivered the tray down to Rory in her lifeguard chair. But knowing that Stevie and my dad were watching from the window, Rory promptly threw the poem— unopened— onto the deck and returned her attention back to the pool. It took a few more (appropriate) attempts before Rory agreed to go out with Stevie. There was even some gentle nudging from Grandma Gloria, who told Rory and the other lifeguards, including her sister Jeanmarie, at one Wednesday Night Dinner, "One of you girls is going to marry Stevie". By 1992, Stevie and Rory were finally married, their unconventional 'meet-cute' securing a permanent place in the Palms matchmaking hall of fame.

There would be many other staff pairings over the years. John Vitolo met and married his snack bar countermate Caroline Taylor. John's brother, bartender Billy Vitolo, found his future wife in waitress Annika Kaye. And that is not to mention the many members who met and paired off over the years. All told, countless couples traced their beginnings back to the Palms Shore Club, where sun, fun, and youth collided to spark relationships that stood the test of time. With the sheer amount of time staff and members spent there—and the joyful, easygoing atmosphere—it was the perfect place to nurture loving, lasting bonds.

Club PS:
A Nightclub, 90s Style

"Please, please, pleeeease!" I can still hear my older sister Jackie's voice, begging my parents to let her go. Club PS did sound pretty cool, even to my seven-year-old self: an outdoor nightclub on summer weekends with music thumping and crowds dancing under the stars. Of course, now I understand why my parents were hesitant. Club PS nights were much more than music and dancing. My mom spent every weekend on edge, holding her breath that my dad wouldn't get caught in one of the frequent fights or hurt by the drunken, pushy crowd. The last thing she wanted was her innocent eleven-year-old daughter in the middle of it all.

But Jackie was persistent, and it was hard to justify keeping her away from a place that was our family's summer home. So, flanked by a few trusted staff members, and with extra security close by, my pre-teen sister got her wish. She spent a few hours one Saturday night soaking in the loud, chaotic energy of Club PS. Today, she barely remembers going, perhaps a coping mechanism, her young mind blocking out the mayhem. But for that one night, she was a part of my dad's second short-lived masterpiece.

The early 1990s in Brooklyn were all about nightclubs and DJs. And, as always, my dad and Uncle Larry had the best of intentions for bringing that trend to the Palms Shore Club. They pushed Grandpa Bob to give the place a facelift. For thirty years the Palms had been painted simply with a few primary colors. For the new venture, they brought a new look: painting the walls with signature Palms-branded teal, handpainting some of them with vibrant murals, and setting palm trees out front. Then, in the summer of 1994, Club PS was born, "Brooklyn's Only Totally Outdoor Niteclub!"

Every Friday and Saturday night, after the cabana club closed for the day, the atmosphere shifted completely. Gone were the family-friendly egg creams and mahjong tiles; in came the beers, tequila shots and bass-heavy DJ sets. A stocked cash bar kept drinks flowing and music blasted into the humid, salty Sheepshead Bay air, drawing out Brooklyn's youth for the night of dancing and partying in the moonlight. To get it off the ground, my dad and my Uncle Larry hit the nearby beaches, handing out free entry tickets to anyone and everyone, trying to drum up a crowd beyond the cabana club members. And soon, it worked – Club PS was drawing 200 to 300 people each weekend night, becoming a fun, if fleeting, part of the local nightclub scene.

But their ambitions were bigger. My dad and Uncle Larry began collaborating with the popular New York radio stations Z100 and KTU, advertising on-air and booking guest DJs for select nights. And suddenly, Club PS exploded. Twenty-somethings from across

Brochures for Club PS in 1994, advertising the upcoming DJs and performances

Brooklyn lined up all the way down Emmons Avenue– girls tugging down their short dresses and tottering in high heels, guys adjusting the chains hanging over their sleeveless white shirts. They'd hand over their tickets – often to my Aunt Joy (Uncle Larry's wife, who also designed the Club PS logo) – and pour into the club in waves. The crowd reached 500, 700, even close to 1,000 some nights, packed in like sardines on the terraces and around the pool patios. My dad hired more bartenders, beefed up security, and brought in bigger names to entertain: Clarence Clemons, Jay Black and the Americans, The Weather Girls.

He and Uncle Larry were thrilled—it felt like they were on the brink of a true breakout success.

My grandparents were far less convinced. Grandpa Bob and Grandma Gloria never fully supported the Club PS experiment. On weekend nights, they would retreat into their house above the venue and lock the doors tight, while the music blasted and the crowds partied below.

Turns out, my grandparents' instincts on this one were right. The bass-heavy music thumping until two or three in the morning didn't just keep them up—it stirred anger throughout the Sheepshead Bay neighborhood. And the crowds, packed in tight, created the perfect recipe for trouble. It was certainly no place for a ten-year-old. One accidental shove or a glassy-eyed stare in the wrong direction could set off a fight among the drunken young men, all muscle and machismo. Some would break beer bottles to use as a weapon, others would pull out guns that somehow made it past the security at the front. The bouncers, the staff, my dad would all be trying to keep things calm, but by the second season of Club PS, the cops were being called almost every night.

And that was on the nights the club was open. Brooklyn summers are humid, but often unpredictably wet. And in 1995, the rain seemed to come mostly on weekends. With no indoor backup plan, Club PS would have to cancel last-minute, losing money and momentum.

After all the fights, the unpredictability of the weather was the final straw. It became too exhausting, too stressful—and ultimately, unsustainable.

Just like the Disco Hideaway a decade earlier, Club PS had a short life-span, closing in only its third season.

A Supporting Cast of Characters

One of the greatest experiences for a 6-year-old? Finding a secret hiding spot and sneakily eating candy. My favorite hideout was under the weight of women's furs and men's long jackets in the Palms coat check room— a space that doubled as candy storage and my own personal candy stash. Giggling, I'd slowly peel the colorful candy buttons off of the white paper, trying to avoid the bits of paper that would inevitably get stuck. I'd grabbed them from a tin bucket on my way in, with the help of my loyal accomplice: Cutie.

Cutie was the lovely woman who ran coat check and who always let me slip in, unnoticed, between guests. She was one of my favorite people at the Palms—warm, kind, and always doting on us Berfond grandchildren. But she was just one of many. So many staff had been there for years, even decades—always ready with a treat, a helping hand, or a watchful eye. They felt like an extension of the Berfond family.

The truth was, Grandpa Bob and Grandma Gloria could not run the Palms Shore Club alone. It took a team of at least 60 at any given time to keep everything moving: managing the cabana club, running the pools and snack bar, waiting on diners, cooking hundreds of meals, and more. They started with family: Grandma Gloria's mother, Sadie. Grandpa Bob's sister, Sheila. Sheila's children, Philip, Arlyn and Melissa. Cousins Andy and Larry. And of course, their own three sons – my dad Allen, and uncles Larry and Mel – who were raised in the club. They eventually brought in their wives – my mom, Aunt Joy and Aunt Jessica – and, later, us grandkids. Everyone pitched in, often wearing multiple hats. Whatever needed to be done—wrapping baked potatoes in foil, manning the service bar, punching membership cards at the front gate, ringing up lunches at the snack bar, setting up tables, or serving signature dishes at Wednesday and Sunday night dinners—they'd do it. Usually without complaint, often enough with a smile.

Yet the blood family only extended so far. Grandpa Bob and Grandma Gloria were intentional about who they recruited— especially after the professional managers of the first few years proved untrustworthy. They focused on hiring people who were not only competent but who they could truly rely on. There were plenty of young people who rotated through— as cabana boys, snack bar staff, busboys and more— but my grandparents knew they needed a core group of reliable adults leading the charge. And it was an effective strategy. They built a diverse team, many of whom stayed for years, even decades—sometimes bringing their own family members into the Palms community. It became a true family business.

Cutie was one such example. Her mother, Freddie Dinkens, had been there from the very beginning—Grandma Gloria's nanny even before the Palms Shore Club officially opened, helping raise the three boys and keeping them corralled. As my dad and uncles grew older and graduated out of her care, Freddie took on responsibilities at the cabana club: running the women's locker room, cleaning the bathrooms, managing the laundry.

More importantly, she became a sort of nanny for *everyone*. Known to most as Miss Freddie, she was a reliable and grounding presence—salt of the earth—with a sweet, smiling demeanor and a small stature that belied her strength. In the 1980s, she brought in her daughter Onetha, known to all as Cutie, who quickly became a stalwart in the Palms family in her own right, and stayed until the very end. Like her mother, Cutie was both truly kind— especially with children— and completely dependable. She not only ran the coat check room, but jumped in wherever help was needed. A mess in the bathroom? A skirt that needed emergency mending? Someone wanting to book a party when Allen wasn't around? Cutie was on it.

Another all-around fixer? Seymour Messinger. An old friend of Grandpa Bob, Seymour became his right-hand man from the moment the Palms Shore Club opened. Officially, he was in charge of purchasing—ordering the food, drinks, paper goods, and all the supplies that kept the Palms running, from cabana club to catering hall. But like so many others, Seymour wore multiple hats. He often turned around and put those purchases to work himself—managing the snack bar or mixing drinks as a bartender upstairs. (Some even called him "the beverage man.")

He was everywhere, doing whatever Grandpa Bob needed, usually in a matching short-sleeved button-down and with a cigarette also dangling from his mouth. While Grandpa Bob strolled the property like a calm commander, Seymour was constantly in motion—running, sweating, juggling a dozen tasks. Almost everyone who worked at the Palms knew Seymour, and everyone respected him. He was kind, funny, and always ready to lend a hand—though if you forgot to save the leftover dinner rolls for the next party, you'd definitely hear about it. (As busboy Brad Wind recalls). But truly, his good nature was well appreciated and is remembered by all to this day.

Note from 1960s maitre d Mr. Neil Kasman to members, captured in the Palms Shore Tattler

Seymour was almost always at the Palms, and when he was not working, he was often upstairs playing poker with his friend, another good man and Palms fixture, Julie Erlich. The two were inseparable, having worked together for many years. Julie played an integral role in the year-round nightclub – first as Captain starting in the mid 60s and then stepping into the role of maître d' when Neil Kasman left in the mid-1970s. Where Neil had been quiet and a little intimidating – a kind of Frankie Valli figure, all pointy shoes and slicked-back hair – Julie brought a more approachable charisma. Almost always dressed in his tuxedo and bow tie, Julie had a confident swagger and a handsome presence. He was a natural leader for the busy nightclub scene: managing the clamoring crowd, coordinating the entertainment,

1970s maitre d Julie Erlich posing at the Palm Room windows (courtesy of Abbe Elrich Poznak)

and keeping the staff in line, all with style. And since his Palms work was mostly evenings and weekends, it left plenty of time for his other great love—horse racing. On most weekdays, you could find him at Belmont or the Aqueduct Racetrack, placing bets with the same calm precision he brought to the floor at the Palms.

Also part of their crew was Ginger (real name: Louisa Detweiler), a sweet, petite woman who worked at the Palms for twenty-eight years and was just as well-loved as the rest. Most often she ran the coat check at the nightclub, sneaking out for a quick Lucky Strikes smoke break during slower moments. Given the family-friendly environment, she would sometimes bring her granddaughter Noelle along to visit—and eventually, Noelle joined her behind the counter, working at the snack bar for a few summers.

In the later years, when Julie and Ginger had moved on from the Palms, Seymour was likely to be in the company of Grandpa Bob and another Palms regular, Larry Genovese. Known to most as Larry G thanks to the abundance of Larrys in the Berfond orbit, he first joined the Palms in the early 1970s as a bartender in the nightclub.

A Supporting Cast of Characters

Larry G was a character. He had a good heart, but he could be both boisterous and a bit neurotic.

Over time, his job at the Palms became somewhat... unclear. He'd arrive early Saturday mornings to cook up a massive pot of meatballs or some other Italian specialty for the weekend crowd. And beyond that? Well, aside from chasing misbehaving boys around the pool, it was anyone's guess what his official duties were—other than keeping Grandpa Bob company.

The same cannot be said for Rafael Santos, the incredibly hard-working and reliable handyman – and essentially one-man construction crew – for the Palms Shore Club, from the 1970s until its doors closed. All summer long, day-in and day-out, you could find him quietly fixing something around the sprawling complex, dipping in and out of his designated tool room. Grandpa Bob kept him busy as well

HAT CHECK GIRLS

GINGER

also GLORIA ■ MICKEY ■ FLORENCE

Beloved "hat check girl" Ginger, as captured in a 1970 brochure

in the off-season, as Raf took the lead on the many additions and renovations and changes and refreshes that grandpa envisioned over the years, often accompanied by his brother Andre. Each time the snack bar moved. Each time the Palms needed a paint refresh. When a major renovation was required upstate. Raf was the guy to call. He was confident and focused, and though he may swear like a sailor while working and had no love for any cat that got in his way, his handiwork was well-respected.

For many of the smaller to-dos around the Palms, there was also Albert, the maintenance guy. He was another steady presence, starting in the 1980s, always fixing or cleaning something, always helping to keep the place up to Grandpa Bob's exacting standards. Every day, maybe up to sixteen hours per day, he was working hard, helping to maintain the place at Grandpa Bob's level of perfection. Where Grandpa showed more restraint with Raf — whose skills he deeply respected — he let loose on Albert. Despite his thin frame, Albert was strong and resilient, absorbing the intensity of Grandpa's demands — the yelling, the impatience, the insults — often with a smile still on his face.

In his thick Jamaican accent, with a sweeper in hand, he'd shrug and say: "The day is long, my pay is small, I take my time — and f*** them all."

Together, Albert, Rafael and Andre took on the arduous task of washing the entire cabana club every single morning before opening. They'd haul out the hoses and soap, spray down all of the patios and rails, ensuring everything was spotless, all before the cabana boys started pulling out the lounge chairs and tables.

Of course it was critical to have the same level of reliability and diligence in the kitchen, especially in the event hall. A strong, hard-working kitchen crew year-round helped maintain the Palms reputation as a fine dining establishment. First Tommy and then Mr. Ong held the mantle of head chef, each for nearly a decade, maintaining a strict kitchen. They kept the rest of the team under sharp, watchful eyes. Even when they slipped into their native Chinese dialects to yell, their body language — sometimes reinforced with props, like a swiftly banged cleaver — got the message across. They upheld high standards in every way, including cleanliness. For that, they relied on Pappy — a small, smiling man who worked late nights or early mornings, scouring the kitchen spotless. He sometimes even rode the dumbwaiter up and down to bring back heavy pans for cleaning. He barely spoke English, but he was always eager to help the cooks however he could.

A Supporting Cast of Characters

One day in the late 1970s, Pappy accidentally started a small fire while heating hors d'oeuvres in the Luau Room fryer. In his panic, he sprayed the fire extinguisher *into* the fryer — sending a blast of oil flying up to the ceiling and making things worse. The damage was quickly contained, but it wasn't exactly one of the finer moments for such a devoted worker.

In the early 1980s, as the nightclub shifted more toward catering, Mr. Ong left, and the kitchen entered what became known as the Diaz era. Three of the Diaz brothers – Nelson, William and Ariste – had already become critical to the kitchen operations over the years, and Ariste and later, William took on the leadership role. Nelson held the longest tenure of the three, and was known for his cold platters — elaborate, colorful spreads that welcomed guests at every party.

These individuals were just a few of the many people who made the Palms run. Over the years, hundreds of New Yorkers — young and old — served as cooks and cleaners, waitstaff and bartenders, cabana boys and lifeguards, counselors and cashiers, switchboard operators and valet drivers, front gate pass checkers and hat checkers. Most wore multiple hats, returning year after year.

The Palms Shore Club was a family business — and the staff were a vital part of that family. Yes, the expectations were high. But the team rose to meet them, always ready to do what was needed to create a positive guest experience (while managing to have their own fun along the way). They were, without question, the backbone of four decades of a beloved community institution.

A Slow Decline

Monday nights were my dad's night off. Throughout the year, it was the one evening he could reliably be at home in central New Jersey rather than in Brooklyn, working hard to manage the Palms catering hall. We would often go out to a family dinner, perhaps the local Chinese restaurant, and as much as I loved spending time with him at the Palms, it was also a treat to have him home with us. He would relax, laugh and joke with my sister and me, regaling us with stories of demanding customers or misbehaving staff. But even at ten, I could sense a change at those dinners, some signs that business was slowing. I noticed the worry in his eyes, the weight of stress creeping in, the fatigue settling over him.

My cousin Nicole's extravagant 300-person bat mitzvah in October 1998 felt like a last hurrah for our family. When I started preparing for my own bat mitzvah, and my parents shared that it wouldn't be at the Palms, like Nicole's and my sister's, it was both a predictable and devastating moment.

By the 1980s, the times in Brooklyn had begun to change. The middle-class Brooklyn families who were the lifeblood of the Palms cabana club in the 1960s and '70s were now increasingly choosing to spend their summers – and their money – elsewhere. To travel further away, to Florida, to California, to Europe and beyond. Some loyal members stayed on, bringing their children and grandchildren to relive familiar traditions; but for many, Sheepshead Bay was no longer the center of their lives. Their worlds were widening.

Lifestyles, too, were shifting. More women were entering the workforce, including married mothers, the core of the Palms cabana club clientele. No longer were these women searching for a way to occupy their summer weekdays, or a place to spend the hot days with their friends and children by the pool. The appeal of full-time cabana club membership began to wane.

These cultural changes marked the end of an era. Cabana clubs across the New York region started to feel the impact, struggling and fighting to maintain their members. Even the Palms' longtime rival, the Deauville, fell into bankruptcy in the mid 1980s. The bank brought in a management company, which tried to lure new members by targeting Palms customers with 15-20% discounts if they switched clubs. Naturally, Grandpa Bob was furious when he found out.

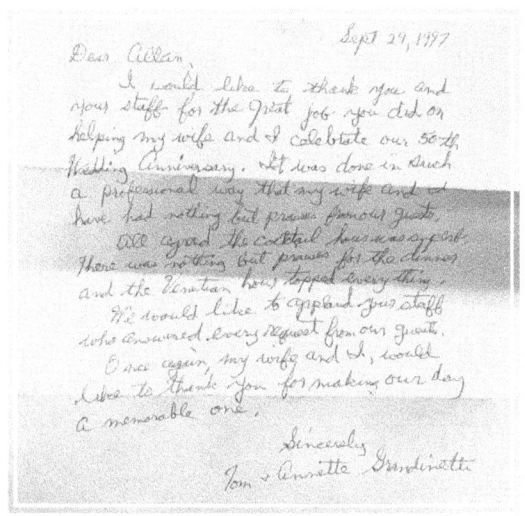

Post-celebration 'Thank You' notes sent to my dad by Palms customers over the years

Already somewhat litigious, and now with his son Mel freshly graduated from New York Law School, Grandpa had the perfect in-house attorney. With his father's encouragement, Uncle Mel opened his own law practice – conveniently handling the many lawsuits lodged both by and against the Palms.

When Grandpa discovered the Deauville's tactics, he immediately wanted to sue. Uncle Mel quickly got smart on 'intentional interference with contractual business relations.' To gather evidence, they sent trusty Frankie Cass to the Deauville posing as an interested customer. Sure enough, he came back with a written contract offering a "special discount" for Palms members. Uncle Mel filed the lawsuit, and within days, a settlement was reached and the poaching stopped. The Deauville soon went under anyway, like so many others, its building eventually replaced by a movie theater.

The Palms Shore Club held on through the 1980s, buoyed in part by its strong catering business, loyal customers, and the Berfond family's tireless efforts to stay on top of the trends, to innovate, to keep their kingdom alive. And the closing of other cabana clubs did bring in some new customers, including a few gangs of families eager to hold onto the way of life a little longer.

But by the mid-1990s, even the Palms' own numbers were dwindling. Cabana club membership had dropped to around 800 or 900, just half of its 1,500 capacity, and nowhere near enough to cover rising real estate taxes and utility costs.

At the same time, the catering business was facing its own challenges. For years, the Palms had been *the* place for weddings in Sheepshead Bay—offering on-site ceremonies, lavish cocktail hours by the pool, and an elegant experience for a reasonable price. But by the 1990s, other venues started to make significant investments, creating higher-end alternatives, and the competition for events grew (from Russos on the Bay to the El Caribe). Without a strong off-season revenue base, there were real financial challenges.

Still, the Berfonds were not ones to give up. In the mid-to-late 1990s, my grandparents, my dad, and my uncles were brainstorming ways to bring in revenue – renovating the front entrance, adding a new room, trying to modernize. My dad even sent some waitresses to competing venues as "secret shoppers," to scope out menus and gather ideas. But it was hard to find what would really make the difference.

Then came the bigger swings. They explored the idea of opening a restaurant on the marina, as few businesses were taking advantage of the beautiful waterfront at that time. They even hired an architect to draw up plans. But the city denied the proposal, citing, of course, inadequate parking. Another idea was to build an ice skating rink to bring customers in the winter, but that too met regulatory roadblocks.

Eventually, the Berfond family faced reality. The time had come to sell—to accept that the neighborhood, the families, and people's habits had changed. And with that decision, they prepared to close the book on a remarkable four-decade journey.

Labor Day, September 7, 1998 was the final day of Palms' last summer season. While the catering hall would stay open a few more months, this was the true finale for Brooklyn's summer home. Fittingly, it came with a touch of drama: a powerful windstorm – a *derecho*—swept through New York City that day, bringing tornado-like gusts that wreaked havoc across the region, including at the Palms. Mats and lounge chairs flew through the air, and the pools churned like stormy seas.

But the staff and members who showed up that day leaned into the chaos as a catharsis. People surfed across waterlogged decks on lounge-chair mats, hurled condiments across the tennis courts, laughed, and shouted through the wind. The mess no longer mattered.

At the end of the day, our extended family took refuge in the snack bar, pushing together tables for a final, delicious, bittersweet feast. Somehow the mayhem turned what could have felt like a funeral for the Palms Shore Club into a celebration of its life—a fitting, free-spirited send-off for this truly unforgettable Brooklyn institution.

The Palms Shore Club

Dana Borell address the Manhattan Beach Community Group about the possibility of a summer flea market on Emmons Avenue.

So Long to the Palms Shore Club?

By Helen Klein

Is the sun setting at last on the Palms Shore Club?

Located at 3128 Emmons Avenue, the club, a cabana club and catering hall, has been a Sheepshead Bay institution for years. However, it now appears that the days of the venerable club are numbered, with rumors abounding that the property is in the process of being sold.

Spokespeople for the club would neither confirm nor deny the rumors. However, while Melvin Berfond, the club's attorney, would say only, "I am not authorized to discuss it with you," when asked if the club would be closing in the near future, an unidentified employee of the establishment noted, "Where's the story? Everybody knows that the club may close, that the land may be sold. They know it here, and they know it in Florida."

Pat Singer, the executive director of the Brighton Neighborhood Association, is one of those who tried to book the club for an event next year, but was told that the club was not taking reservations after January.

"I make a dinner there, every year, in March," Singer recounted, "and they told me, when I called to book, that they would be closing as of January. It's kind of sad."

Singer said that she understood that the owners, "had been negotiating to sell the site for a long time. They finally have someone interested."

Asked if she knew what was planned for the location, Singer replied, "I have heard talk of maybe building some sort of housing, there. But," she continued, "nobody knows. I don't know.

"Communities move on," Singer continued. "Hopefully, 10 years from now, we'll see something exciting in its place."

Ed Eisenberg, a member of Community Board 15, noted that, if the Palms Shore Club indeed closes, it would be almost the end of an era. "What's left?" he asked. "La Mer is gone. If the Palms Shore Club closes, there will only be the El Caribe."

Eisenberg recalled that, approximately a year ago, the Berfond family, which owns the Palms Shore Club, had come before CB 15 requesting a variance to build an ice skating rink at the site, which would have increased its year-round use, and increased the profit generated by the 60,000-square-foot cabana club, which is open only three months a year. However, while the board approved the application, Eisenberg said the application had run into difficulties further along in the approval process, and never came to fruition.

Bay News article in May 1998 speculating on the impending closure of the Palms Shore Club

EPILOGUE

The wide inviting front steps are gone. As is the classic and instantly recognizable facade, with its curved windows and stucco walls. You can still find a version of that facade about a quarter of a mile down Emmons Avenue, at the Miramar Yacht Club that my grandfather horse-traded for all those years ago. But twenty-five years after its closing, the Palms Shore Club is gone without a trace. In its place stands – yes, you guessed it – condos. White-washed apartment buildings and parking spaces now fill the stretch between Emmons Avenue and Sheepshead Bay. There's no sign of the forty years of history that unfolded there: the swim days and Wednesday night barbecues, the weddings and bar and bat mitzvahs, the Italian festivals and comedy shows, the dalliances and fistfights, the lives that were shaped and changed at the Palms Shore Club.

Well, maybe one trace remains: a rusted fence on the far right end of the property, the only visible marker of what once stood there.

On an April day in 2024, my mom pulled over the car and let my dad and me step out. The condo entry was locked, but as luck would have it, a car pulled up at that moment and opened the access gates. We slipped through. It was unremarkable, and yet somehow, remarkable, with my dad pointing out what used to be where. My own sense of direction was completely off; I couldn't quite map the memories and photos in my mind onto the space before us. Everything felt smaller, stranger. But my dad still saw it as his home.

We couldn't go far, hemmed in by the buildings and parking lots, but we did make it down to the water. The fishing boats were still there, waiting to be hired for the day. Across the bay, Kingsborough Community College still stood. It was windy but sunny, and with the smell of the salt in the air, we were transported back to those final days of the Palms.

The Palms Shore Club officially closed in January 1999, after a culminating New Year's Eve celebration. It was the end of an era.

Over its nearly forty-year history, thousands upon thousands of people passed through the Palms. Some came only once or twice—to attend a wedding, a bar or bat mitzvah—and carried away memories of delicious food and a great time with friends and family. To this day, a member of the Berfond family can hardly go a week without meeting someone who remembers the Palms Shore Club, whether at a party at my dad's new catering hall in New Jersey – the eponymously-named Palms Plaza – or simply while out to dinner at a local restaurant.

But many others had deeper connections. From cabana club members who were there from start to finish to staff who worked at the Palms for ten, twenty, thirty years or more—the club was their home. It was a community where they felt they belonged, a place where they met lifelong friends or partners. Even now, when asked about their time at the Palms, nearly everyone says the same thing: it was one of the best times of their lives—a time they wish they could go return to.

Even the staff, who certainly worked hard, felt that sense of belonging. They worked alongside their parents, siblings, cousins, and friends. They were teased, occasionally yelled at by Grandpa Bob—sometimes loudly—but they were part of his extended family.

It was also a place where people discovered themselves: their interests, their ambitions, their work ethic. The lessons learned at the Palms about hard work, teamwork, and pride carried into their lives long after they left, passed down to their own children. For many, when they tell the story of who they became, the Palms is part of that story.

Grandpa Bob passed away in 2001, just two years after the Palms Shore Club shut its gates. They said it was lung cancer, but it might just as easily have been from a broken heart – though he would never have admitted to either. Grandma Gloria passed away seven years later, in 2008. Both were seventy-three, both too young.

EPILOGUE

They never had the chance to document their story or the history of the Palms Shore Club. But I hope they understood the significance of what they built—the community they created, the memories that still endure, and the lasting power of their legacy.

There are not as many places like the Palms Shore Club today. There exist few spaces where people can truly build and be part of a community. The world has gotten more complicated, and we have become more disconnected.

But these memories are powerful reminders of what's possible. Reading and hearing so many of these beautiful stories, understanding the role a place like the Palms played, has given me hope. There is still a craving for connection, a nostalgia strong enough to pull us back together. And the Palms' legacy, even if accidental, can serve as a blueprint for how we can do it.

Acknowledgements

This isn't just my story - it is the story of the Palms Shore Club family.

First and foremost, I want to thank all 900+ members of the Palms Shore Club community who posted your memories on Facebook, connected with each other, and shared your excitement and appreciation. It was truly this engagement by hundreds of staff and cabana club members and guests that inspired me to document the unique history of the Palms. I tried my best to include many of these names, stories and photos in these pages, and even those not cited explicitly were integral: It is this treasure trove that allowed me to really bring the Palms' story to life. In particular, thank you to Eddie Reavan and Barry Weinstein, for serving as Administrators of the Facebook page and catalyzing all of this.

This book ended up being more of an undertaking than I expected, and I could not have completed it without Lisa Pulitzer, my editor and coach over the past year and a half. Thank you Lisa, for being such a champion of this project! And I would not have met Lisa if not for Sarah Bullen and her Writing Room Retreat. The week I spent in Tuscany with Sarah and an incredible group of writers was exactly the space and guidance I needed to get started and begin to make sense of the trove of input and research about the Palms.

To continue to make progress over the year, I so appreciated the Brooklyn Women Writers Group - the space and wonderful women who created a structure and motivation to keep going. And then a huge thank you to Stephanie Larkin and the team at Red Penguin for helping me to make this into a real book, a dream I have had since I was young.

This project was really only possible through the first-hand stories of those who spent time at the Palms Shore Club. Beyond the Facebook group, thank you to all of those who got on the phone with me to relive your memories in even more depth: my extended family, including Arlyn Weinberg Brenner-Blum, Philip Weinberg and Melissa Goidel, Larry Berfond and Andy Berfond. And many others who were part of the broader Palms family: Faith Cohen,

Acknowledgements

Stevie and Rory Efron, Lonny Friedland, Alan Horowitz, Ronald Kestenbaum, Rachael Komissaroff, Brian Lawrence, Nancy, Perry H Rausher, Eddie Reavan, David Schub, Jeff Siber, Cindy Solomon, Barry Weinstein, Letitia Yemma, Eric Yorke.

Hats off to Anthony Scire, aka "Skeery Jones" of the Elvis Duran and the Morning Show on Z100 New York, who not only recounted his memories of the Palms in impressive detail, but wrote the wonderful Foreword that I know will resonate with so many. Thank you again.

The time that Skeery and so many others were willing to put into this project is a true testament to the meaningful legacy of the Palms.

I so appreciate my Berfond cousin crew, with whom I spent the 1990s running around the Palms Shore Club, splashing in the pools, and creating memories that were so unique to our family. Nicole and Jenine, thank you for helping to surface so many of those memories. And to my younger cousins - Jake, Lindsey, Sarah, Alex, and Justine - thank you for all of the support. This project would not have been possible without them and the rest of my family, and I cannot express enough appreciation.

Enormous gratitude to my mom, Barbie, who provided a constant source of encouragement, in addition to all of the input and reviews and logistical help over the past two years, and to my sister, Jackie, who read drafts, provided valuable feedback, and provided the needed boosts of motivation.

And perhaps most of all, I want to thank my dad, Allen, my Uncle Mel, and my Uncle Larry, who sadly passed away in 2019. This is really their story—the story of them, their parents and the legacy they created. During the writing of this book, Uncle Mel regaled me with decades of tales about growing up at the Palms Shore Club and generously reviewed early drafts with a thoughtful, careful eye. My dad was my constant source of information, sharing memories over dinners and long drives, answering my endless questions, calling on friends to contribute their own stories, and proudly talking about the book to anyone who would listen, which was reason enough for me to keep going through this journey.

www.ingramcontent.com/pod-product-compliance
Lightning Source LLC
Chambersburg PA
CBHW042111190326
41540CB00003B/3